ENVIRONMENT, SPACE, PLACE

VOLUME 15 / ISSUE 1 / SPRING 2023

Environment, Space, Place (ISSN 2066-5377) is published twice a year in the spring and fall by the University of Minnesota Press, 111 Third Avenue South, Suite 290, Minneapolis, MN 55401-2520. http://www.upress.umn.edu

Postmaster: Send address changes to *Environment, Space, Place*, University of Minnesota Press, 111 Third Avenue South, Suite 290, Minneapolis, MN 55401-2520.

Essays (between 6,000 and 10,000 words) should be prepared using *Chicago Manual of Style* endnotes. Authors' names should not appear on manuscripts; instead, please include a separate document with the author's name and address and the title of the article and an abstract with your electronic submission. Authors should not refer to themselves in the first person in the submitted text or notes if such references would identify them; any necessary references to the author's previous work, for example, should be in the third person. Submissions and editorial queries should be sent to paddockt1@southernct.edu.

Books or films for review should be addressed to
Jeffrey Webb
Review Editor, *Environment, Space, Place*
Department of History & Political Science
Huntington University
2303 College Avenue
Huntington, IN 46750

Address subscription orders, changes of address, and business correspondence (including requests for permission and advertising orders) to *Environment, Space, Place*, University of Minnesota Press, 111 Third Avenue South, Suite 290, Minneapolis, MN 55401-2520.

Subscriptions: For our current subscription rates please see our website: http://www.upress.umn.edu. *Environment, Space, Place* is available online through Project MUSE at http://muse.jhu.edu.

ENVIRONMENT, SPACE, PLACE

VOLUME 15 / ISSUE 1 / SPRING 2023

Clashing Globes: Images of the Earth and   1
Heidegger's Thinking of Modernity
    SIMON FERDINAND

Sonic Histories: Reckoning with Race through Campus Soundscapes   32
    TYLER KINNEAR, ROBERT HUNT FERGUSON,
    AND JESSICA M. HAYDEN

Reinhabiting Ecotopia: Weaving the Threads   66
of People, Place, and Possibilities
    RANDALL AMSTER

Wild Design: Gambiarra, Complexity and Responsibility   88
    MONAÍ DE PAULA ANTUNES

Towards a Newer Analytical Frame for Theorizing Ethnic   116
Enclaves in Urban Residential Spaces: A Critical Dialectical
Approach in Relational-Spatiality
    NAWAL SHAHARYAR

Book Reviews

Cartographic Memory: Social Movement Activism   139
and the Production of Space by Juan Herrera
    REVIEWED BY AÍDA R. GUHLINCOZZI

The Porch: Meditations on the Edge of Nature by Charlie Hailey   142
    REVIEWED BY BRUCE B. JANZ

The Nature of Space by Milton Santos   147
   REVIEWED BY DAVE McLAUGHLIN

Spatializing Culture: The Ethnography of Space   151
and Place by Setha Low
   REVIEWED BY CARLOS J. L. BALSAS

Clashing Globes

Images of the Earth and Heidegger's Thinking of Modernity

SIMON FERDINAND[1]

Abstract

Visual representations of the whole earth permeate modern cultures, shaping how societies imagine globalization and planetary ecological derangement. To explore the complex ways in which these images configure human attitudes toward environments, this essay attends to a series of hegemonic representations of the earth from diverse situations and stages of modernity in conjunction with ideas drawn from Martin Heidegger's ontological philosophy. I proceed from the insight that for Heidegger modernity is not a singular condition, but entails two contrary determinations of being: "machination," in which detached subjects reshape an objectified world, and "enordering," in which fungible and flexible resources circulate endlessly around a closed global space. Taking up these divergent concepts, my argument accentuates basic differences in how the earth has been disclosed in representation over the course of modern history. Through close analyses of world maps from the early modern Netherlands; chalkboard globes from nineteenth-century schoolrooms; and the contemporary geospatial application Google Earth, I show how global visions both articulate and complicate Heidegger's thinking of machination and enordering. Far from being the culmination of a singular modernity, images of the earth reveal and reinforce a discordant global condition, riven by clashing, equally total disclosures of the world.

INTRODUCTION

Images of the earth, globe, world, and planet are so pervasive in contemporary media, culture, and advertising as to have sunk into the unobtrusive, largely unscrutinized backdrop to everyday life.[2] Skeletal graticules promote banks and haulage companies. Whole earth favicons emblazon browser tabs. Fragile planets figure on protest banners. Spinning globes introduce newsroom broadcasts. Such visions have assumed a heightened significance in the current moment of planetary ecological derangement and afflicted geopowers, not despite their being so commonplace, but rather precisely because they are ostensibly trivial. From the unremarked thresholds of our attention, images of the earth mediate how societies imagine climate heating and other unfolding planetary upheavals precipitated by fossil capitalism. Endowed with these subtle capacities, they have been enrolled in support of various, often competing agendas and embody starkly divergent apprehensions of the "globe" at stake in global environmental change. Yet whether they cast the planet as a borderless commons or agglomeration of resources, pliant geode or elemental manifold, images of the earth have at least this much in common: that they take a stand on the character of terrestrial existence and beckon onlookers into entering specific relationships with earthly totality.

As Jennifer Wenzel has observed, a frequent maneuver in contemporary critical discourse is "to invoke the *globe* and *global* as the index of a hegemonic epistemology . . . against which suppressed or emergent utopian alternatives can be articulated."[3] Although the intention behind this move is to preserve diverse cultural visions of earth from being subsumed under prevailing constructions of globality, taking the hegemonic modern globe as a critical foil for various counter-imaginaries in this way risks flattening the complexities of dominant global images. Indeed, global visions are often construed as paradigms of objectification and estrangement, inspiring "an intoxicating sense of a total overview, global and dominating."[4] Estrangement and objectification are crucial to the story of how the earth has been represented in modernity, to be sure, and feature prominently in what follows. But my claim is that they are *just* part of the story. Modern cultures apprehend earthly space in ways that exceed critical tropes of the estranged total overview, which, though indispensable, neglect other dimensions of global spatialities.

If existing work on images of the earth tends to contrast a dominant global overview with marginalized alternative perspectives, this essay explores disjunctures *within* hegemonic Western traditions of global representation.[5] I am referring to differences not of rhetoric, formal presentation, or overt political agenda, but of underlying, largely implicit understandings of what global space fundamentally *is*. To show how dominant modes of representing the earth diverge at this basic, ontological level, I approach them in conjunction with ideas drawn from the philosophy of Martin Heidegger, the theoretical source for many critical accounts of dominant global visions. Indeed, in attempting to grasp how images of the earth configure human attitudes toward environments, commentators working across various disciplines and critical perspectives have found an irresistible point of reference in Heidegger's searching reflections on planetary technicity and modern representationalism.[6] The well-known essay "The Age of the World Picture" (1938) is especially resonant in this context, its very title implying that global representation, over and above all other phenomena of modern history, defines the age and so gives it its name. A number of scholars have taken up Heidegger's description of the objectification of the world in this essay to claim that global representations encapsulate modern societies' detachment from and domination over terrestrial environments.[7] This is not to suggest that all writing on global images proceeds in a Heideggerian vein; far from it. Still, even where scholars of global visions do not invoke Heidegger explicitly, his thinking of modernity and the world picture often exerts an indirect influence through the anthropologist Tim Ingold's much-cited essay "Globes and Spheres," which, as Cory Austin Knudson persuasively argues, "rather straightforwardly ventriloquizes Heidegger's anxieties" concerning humanity's estrangement from the earth figured as a globe.[8]

My contribution to this discussion unfolds from a recognition that despite the clear resonances of Heidegger's work with the theme of global representation, especially in "The Age of the World Picture," the ways in which his philosophy actually bears upon images of the earth are more elusive and fraught than appearances might initially suggest. Several issues might be mentioned in this regard, but in this essay I am concerned with a problematic arising from how Heidegger's thinking of modernity is to be interpreted. A number of commentaries on Heidegger assume that his later writings address a cohesive ontological condition—a singular modernity, as it were.[9] In this secondary literature, Heidegger's descriptions of various modern processes and phenomena are packaged together as belonging to this one determination of being, often defined in terms of "enframing" (the most common

English translation of *Gestell*, Heidegger's term for the technological casting of being). Even some of Heidegger's most perspicacious readers gloss over key complexities and disjunctures in what they see as his narrative of modernity-as-enframing, which Thomas Sheehan goes so far as to call it a "Solzhenitsyn-like jeremiad against modernity *au large.*"[10]

Eschewing this received grasp of Heidegger's thinking of modernity in the singular, I take my bearings from revisionist readings of his later writings, which stress that for Heidegger modernity is marked by not one, but two determinations of being.[11] Rather than reducing the diverse phenomena of modern history to a single ontological disclosure, Heidegger actually traces an unfolding rift *within* modernity, whereby one, established casting of being is progressively overtaken by another. In the first of these ontologies, which Heidegger designates *Machenschaft* (machination), existence is disclosed in terms of self-encapsulated Cartesian subjects imposing their will on "makeable" objects, defined by their capacity to be reconstituted through external imposition. Although I go on to query Heidegger's periodizations, his history of being describes how machination arose in the sixteenth century and remained dominant into the twentieth. He names the second ontology Gestell, which in this article I have chosen to translate as "enordering" for reasons set out later on. Within the horizon of enordering, the distinction between subject and object wanes. People, things, and environments show up instead as "standing reserve," flexible and fungible resources that are endlessly switched and driven about to perpetuate and optimize technosocial systems. On my reading, Heidegger implies that this second ontology began taking hold in the decades following World War Two.

Taking up these concepts in a discussion of images of the earth, I realize, involves extracting them from Heidegger's wider thinking of modernity, much of which I leave aside.[12] Still, my aim is not to explore the permutations of the global in Heideggerian philosophy, but to use his meditations on machination and enordering to discriminate between different ontologies at stake in global representation.[13] Drawing on Heidegger's intuition of the ontological fissures running through modern history, my argument emphasizes how images of the earth, far from being the culmination of a singular modernity, reveal and reinforce a discordant, even aporetic ontological condition, riven by clashing, equally total determinations of being. In making that argument, I analyze a series of global representations drawn from various situations of modernity, showing how they apprehend the earth in ways that both parallel and complicate Heidegger's thought. To accentuate basic differences in how the earth has been disclosed over modern history and stress how even dominant geographical traditions are refracted through fundamentally discrepant global visions, I have chosen to look at images of the earth that were made centuries apart and each reinforced hegemonic perceptions of earthly space in their time. Far from exploiting these cases merely to illustrate or concretize Heideggerian ontology, I approach them as theoretical objects, able to complicate and contribute to the philosophical discourses posed alongside them.

This remainder of this essay is structured as follows. First, I explore how the dynamics of machination played out in the cartographic culture of the early modern Netherlands. Having explained Heidegger's thinking of machination, I show how Dutch world maps and global images positioned the human as a detached ocular subject, set above an objectified world. Whereas for Heidegger the world under machination is fundamentally pliant and amenable to human design, I argue that this "makeability" was fully established in global representation only centuries later, in slated globes: blank chalkboard spheres popular in nineteenth-century schoolrooms. Presenting earth as a *tabula rasa* inviting reinscription, slated globes literalize the modern world's malleability.

The second half of the essay turns to enordering. After describing this disclosure, I show how it is articulated in the geospatial application Google Earth. Embedding networked users in a digital globe augmented with their media, the program disperses subjectivity through the world against which it was previously defined. A teeming mosaic of photographs, the program also embodies the standing reserve's restlessness and replaceability. That said, I stress how Google Earth tempers Heidegger's absolute conception of enordering. Whereas he describes enordering as a system of global fungibility and functionality, so encompassing and hyperconnected that space and distance evaporate, Google Earth is not only littered with anomalies, profanities, and glitches that confound utility, but asserts the continuing importance of space and location amid frenzied circulation and replacement.

In disclosing the space of world, images of the earth articulate basic possibilities for being, thought, and action that people and polities might act upon according to their political situation and interests. To show how this is as true today as in any other phase in the history of global representation, I close the essay by reflecting on how the global visions implicit in machination and enordering are now playing out in the context of ecological politics.

MACHINATION

In distinguishing between machination and enordering in line with recent rereadings of Heidegger, it is important to note that Heidegger does not explicitly do so himself. The difference between them is not a programmatic distinction, but an inchoate divergence that must be extrapolated from his writings. It would therefore be uncharitable to claim that commentators get Heidegger wrong in blurring machination and enordering. My impression is that, although he sensed a shift in the postwar period, the ambiguities of the transition meant that Heidegger did not quite take the step of announcing a new dispensation of being.

Nonetheless, his writings indicate an unfolding ontological break within modernity. This section describes the first of the two disclosures that emerge from that divergence: "machination," Heidegger's name for the casting of being that prevailed from the seventeenth into the twentieth century. Although ordinarily machination signifies "plotting," Heidegger explains that he intends the word "to point to *making*": it names "an interpretation of beings which brings their makeability to the fore."[14] This sense of the world's malleability arises from a bifurcation of beings into objects and subjects. In "The Age of the World Picture," Heidegger argues that this split is crystallized in the category of *representation*. Although the modern concept of representation "is first expressed by the [Latin] word *repraesetatio*," its key resonances for Heidegger's argument are pronounced in the German *vorstellen*, literally "fore-placing" or "setting-before." In Heidegger's usage, the term foregrounds relations of estranged confrontation among entities, such as obtain between an image and its observer or maker. Here representation involves "making everything stand over and against [oneself] as object," a process that "masters and proceeds against" things, rather than allowing them to unfold from themselves.[15]

The concept of the world picture emerges from this errant grasp of representation. Although "initially the word 'picture' makes one think of a copy of something," Heidegger takes pains to stress that the world picture is not a picture *of* the world—not a "painting of beings as a whole" such as those discussed in what follows—but "the world grasped as picture."[16] Understanding the "world picture" literally as referring to mimetic depictions, which resemble a reality from which they remain distinct, would obscure the ontological truth that in modernity the world itself takes on the qualities of representation. It becomes a vast objectivity, set before a human viewer. This explains why the world picture is essentially and exclusively modern. Although there were certainly ancient and medieval pictures of the world, Heidegger argues that in these periods there was no world picture, for the character of being was not determined by representation. It would be wrong, then, to imagine a *modern* world picture, one world picture among many. "That the world becomes picture at all," Heidegger claims, "is what distinguishes the essence of modernity."[17]

The age of the world picture is marked by distance, objectification, and malleability. By *distance,* in that representation establishes an ontological and often spatial interval between self and world. This split marks the emergence of the human as an empowered, self-encapsulated subject, imagined as looking in upon or facing up to the world from outside. Heidegger throws this externality into relief by drawing a comparison between modernity and ancient Greece. In this narrative, the Greeks lived among captivating beings and overbearing forces in an encompassing world: "To be looked at by beings, to be included and maintained and so supported by their openness, to be driven about by their conflict and marked by their dividedness, that is the essence of humanity in the great age of Greece."[18] On this telling, whereas the modern subject gazes on the world from without, in this period humanity was drawn into moods, immersed in environments, and in thrall to creatures and things. People may have been "looked upon by beings," but no gaze was set above the world, for being was not determined by detached representational relations.

By *objectification,* in that the emergence of the estranged subject is paralleled by another shift, whereby the multiplicity of beings is recast in terms of objectivity. For Heidegger, this is clearest in modern science. Isolating beings as "objects of explanatory research," scientific practice renders their properties measurable and verifiable: "The objectification of beings is accomplished in a setting-before, a representation, aimed at bringing each being before it in such a way that the man who calculates can be sure—and that means certain—of the being."[19] As present and verifiable, objects have a certain stability, even intransigence. So much is implicit in Francis Bacon's description of the scientific project as that of torturing nature into divulging secrets, which presumes that objects have a constancy and integrity that can be pinned down and revealed. Although Heidegger suggests that being was first fully "defined as the objectness of representation" in Descartes' philosophy of science, he argues that objectivity has come to determine "modernity in general," with beings presencing as objects far beyond the laboratory.[20]

By *malleability,* in that the disclosure of beings as calculable objects renders them liable to human molding, inviting subjects (individual or collective) to reshape the world according to projected designs. Rather than dwell on this city blueprint or those utopian designs, Heidegger emphasizes the mode of presencing that makes the transformative projects of modernity possible. Existence, he writes, "has released itself into sheer accessibility through calculation," establishing a "malleability in which everything is made out ahead of time to be 'do-able' and altogether at our disposal."[21] The stage is set for "unconditioned planning and arranging" and human "dominion over the globe as such."[22]

MAPPING MACHINATION

Having described machination, I now want to show how this ontology played out in the cartographic culture that emerged in the Dutch Republic during the sixteenth and seventeenth centuries. The world picture may not be a picture *of* the world, but many maps and globes presuppose this determination of being and embody its defining characteristics. The explosion of mapping in the early modern Netherlands, I argue, belongs to the crucial opening phase of the age of the world picture. The chronologies align: Heidegger argues that "being was defined as the objectness of representation" in the thought of René Descartes, whose major works were composed amid the flourishing of Dutch map-making.[23] The basic image of the terraqueous globe that predominates today was cemented in this period, absorbing and withstanding subsequent challenges and remediations. If the world was "conquered as picture," to paraphrase Heidegger, then major early battles were fought during the formation of the United Provinces.[24]

The interface between self and world, so crucial for Heidegger's thinking of machination, became newly prominent and problematic in early modern Europe. Colonial contact with the Americas, combined with religious and philosophical controversy, disrupted and denaturalized received conceptions of humanity's place in a created world.[25] Amid this tumult, Dutch mapmakers reimagined how the human self relates to earthly space, offering viewers new subject positions premised on ocular detachment. In Europe in the centuries before the early modern surge in mapmaking, geographical images commonly articulate a sensuous and haptic apprehension of earthbound places.[26] The world maps that emerged from Antwerp and Amsterdam's publishing houses from the sixteenth century onward, in contrast, invite onlookers into a zenithal viewing position, elevated above and beyond a world that has been methodically flattened and marshaled into conformity with one, synoptic vision.

This viewing position, I claim, institutes a split between the detached subject and objectified world such as Heidegger describes. At the onset of Dutch cartographic modernity, the relationship between self and world is imagined in terms of elevation and externality: the world mapped was the world seen from on high. To do justice to critical cartographers' hard-won gains against myths of objectivity, I should stress that maps are not transparent windows but complex sign systems: there is no vantage point from which the earth resembles its cartographic image. But that says little about how mapped space has been culturally understood, not least in the early modern Netherlands, in which the difference between self and world was imagined through tropes of flight, height, and spectacle. I will name three such tropes, parsing how each configures attitudes toward earthly space.

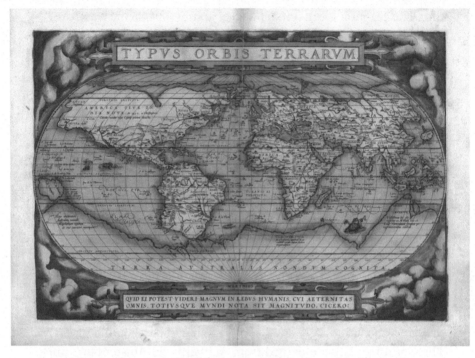

Figure 1. *Typus orbis terrarum*, Abraham Ortelius, 1570. Courtesy of the Library of Congress, Parallel Histories: Spain, the United States, and the American Frontier.

First, the *Typus orbis terrarum,* Abraham Ortelius's world map of 1570, represents global space girded by billowing clouds, as if from an airborne platform (Figure 1). The atlas to which it belongs includes a poem by the diplomat Adolf van Meetkercke, which describes how Apollo had permitted Ortelius to accompany him as he rode his "four-horsed chariot over the air," the mapmaker seeing "regions utterly unknown and situated far below."[27] Initially, this image of an airborne chariot suggests a roving visuality, unshackled from earthly constraints; across Western history, Apollo has embodied a "dream of transcendence" and "will to power" associated with global visions.[28] On reflection, this focalization of the world picture also draws limits. Charged with towing the sun through the sky, Apollo's chariot is bound to an interminable cycle of sunrise and sundown. Further, in Van Meetkercke's rhapsody, Apollo allows Ortelius to ride with him only temporarily, suggesting that the world map, far from defining a properly human subject position, offers a fleeting glimpse of a god's inhuman vision. And the idea of flying beside Apollo inevitably recalls the cautionary tale of Icarus, who fell emulating Apollonian transcendence.

Second, Gerhard Mercator opened his *Atlas* by promising to "set before your eyes, the whole world," presented "as from a loftie watch tower" (Hexham's 1636 translation of Mercator's "*veluti ex alta animi specula*").[29] The image is ambivalent; the tower might be construed as benevolently watching over the world or a sign of occupation. Regardless of this, Mercators stress on the tower's loftiness—which connotes not just elevation but performed distinction—separates its sentries from earthbound people and things, which are miniaturized and flattened in the manner of the objectified world picture. The conceit of a tower so tall that it overlooks, impossibly, the entire world recalls the Tower of Babel, which was also global in that it was built by a united humanity. In Mercator's time, God's leveling of that edifice was interpreted as punishing human pride. The elevated power signified by this image, then, is shadowed by anxiety that to vertically transgress humanity's earthbound condition is to court disaster.

Third, many early modern atlases bear the word *theatrum* in their titles, the earliest being Ortelius's *Theatrum Orbis Terrarum* (theater of the earthly sphere), in which the *Typus* appears. The world becomes a stage across which human history plays out, viewers its audience. Unlike the watchtower and aerial chariot, the theater is grounded and horizontally orientated. Although that might suggest a flat ontology, images of theatrical spectatorship, arches, and curtains cement a gap between spectator and spectacle. Some early modern maps and prospects are shown bordered by drapes and stage curtains, amplifying and dramatizing map frames' separating function.[30] Yet this metaphor can also soften the division between viewer and world. Rendered literally, the Greek *théatron* might mean a "place for viewing," suggesting "rational detachment," but the early modern stage often featured rowdy exchanges among players and the crowd, which would only settle into a docile audience in the nineteenth century.[31] If the image of the theater casts the earth as a detached spectacle, from this slant it also affords the possibility of unruly commerce between self and world.

Despite hinting at countervailing possibilities, these images of a chariot, tower, and theater set viewers at an imagined remove from earthly space, which dovetails closely with Heidegger's concept of representation as "placing before," whereby an objectified world is set "over and against" a human subject. The triumph of vorstellen in Dutch mapmaking is clearest not in maps themselves but depictions showing the subject facing the mapped globe from a third viewpoint. In particular, I am thinking of the title page to Gerhard Mercator's posthumous *Atlas Sive Cosmographicæ Meditationes De Fabrica Mvndi Et Fabricati Figvra* (Atlas or cosmographic meditations on the creation of the world and the image of the created) of 1595. In titling this compendia of maps *Atlas,* Mercator conceptually consolidated a visual genre that has retained that name for more than four centuries. The engraving on its title page depicts the mythological figure of Atlas, who is shown braced in a Renaissance portico with two globes (Figure 2). Mercator is not simply parading his classical learning. Following Ayesha Ramachandran, who argues that the figure is "utterly unlike conventional allegorical depictions of Atlas," I claim that by reworking the traditional Atlas, Mercator's title page encapsulates a newly detached and assertive human bearing toward the world.[32]

Most ancient and Renaissance renditions of Atlas present the Titan as an exhausted elderly man straining under the weight of the cosmos, which suggests an agonized resignation to one's place in a received or imposed order, or simply to life's hardships and responsibilities. Atlas was condemned to his task after revolting against the Olympian gods, suggesting that attempts to impose one's will on the universe only lead to further submission to it. Mercator's Atlas, by contrast, is a muscled geometer, cooly measuring a globe with a compass. Whereas the conventional Atlas looks away from the sphere, which is manifest to him through weight exerted on his shoulders, here Atlas holds and visually contemplates it. The globe is at his disposal. Further, if in ancient mythology and visual culture Atlas carries the heavens or cosmos, Mercator seems to be modulating the figure toward modern variations in which he is laden with the terraqueous globe instead. The globe at Atlas's feet features oceans and landmasses; that in his hand is a bare graticule. Far from being subordinate to the heavy heavens, this Atlas can seek to understand—and potentially remake—his own conditions down on earth.

This is more than simply a divergent visual rendering of an otherwise stable mythological figure. In the early modern period as today,

Figure 2. Title page (detail), *Atlas Sive Cosmographicæ Meditationes De Fabrica Mvndi Et Fabricati Figvra*, Gerhard Mercator, 1595. Courtesy of the Library of Congress, Rare Book and Special Collections Division.

Atlas was widely identified as a straining Titan, compelled to carry the cosmos. In his introduction, though, Mercator explains that his *Atlas* refers to another ancient Atlas: "a most skillfull astrologer" and the first person "that disputed the Sphœre . . . excelling in erudition, humanitie, and wisedome." The prototypical humanist, this other Atlas was a fitting model for the subject of Dutch cartographic culture. By presenting this obscure Atlas as an alternative to the burdened Titan, Mercator founded the atlas, that quintessential genre of world-picturing, on a radical re- casting of the human as newly autonomous and assertive. In his lone confrontation with the terrestrial globe, Atlas condenses the detached and confrontational relations between self and world named by machination. The human becomes subject, an encapsulated self, abstracted from the quiddity and flux down on earth. Atlas does not inhabit the world, but peers at it from a place outside, as if through parted stage curtains. And the world, whether flattened out through cartographic projection or conjured as a globe, becomes an objectified, pictorial surface.

As Tim Ingold has argued, once the earth appears in this way—as a face or something faced up against—then we are already amid the transformative programs of modernity.[33] The face of the earth is a surface primed for inscription. Indeed, for Heidegger, the world's "makeability" is the defining feature of machination. Aspects of my analysis seem to support this; consider how Mercator's Atlas looms over the world, which, objectified and available, appears primed for remaking. Yet despite appearances, the transformative dimensions of world-picturing remain inchoate in early modern cartographic culture. Atlas brims with Promethean energy and Mercator describes the world as "this Fabrick," a product of "workmanship."[34] Yet here the worldmaking is performed not by the human subject, but the Christian God, whom Mercator calls "the workmaster of all things."[35]

Early modern Dutch mapmaking might embody the world picture's distance and objectification, but in this period the sense of the world's fundamental amenability to human intervention is still emergent. Although Mercator's fabricated world anticipates visions of human mastery, centuries would pass before the human "makeability" of beings would be fully articulated in global representation. I therefore track forward here to the nineteenth century, which saw the spread of so-called slated globes. Unlike conventional globes, which are covered in gores representing landforms, oceans, and geobodies, slated globes are blank spheres, often finished with slate liquid or powder, allowing them to be drawn upon with chalk. Some include continental outlines; others are featureless orbs. Consider a slated globe kept at the Smithsonian Museum (Figure 3). Save for some nicks and traces of chalk, the sphere is pristine, awaiting inscription. Its surface presents no impediments (nor stimuli) to imagined journeys or designs, no bodies or forces for aspirant worldmakers to account for. Most slated globes were pedagogical tools facilitating demonstration in geography, geometry, and geodesy. They were especially popular in US schoolrooms in the nineteenth

Figure 3. Slated globe, unmarked, probably late-nineteenth century United States. Courtesy of the Division of Medicine and Science, National Museum of American History, Smithsonian Institution.

and twentieth centuries. In this context, Mahshid Mayar persuasively argues, they fulfilled an ideological desire to wipe away entrenched European imperialisms that had thoroughly mapped and occupied the globe, making way for new, American ambitions.[36]

My claim is that slated globes have an ontological significance that goes beyond any one imperial project. A slated globe is the *tabla rasa* par excellence, a surface into which new orders can be impressed without resistance. No longer a great accretion of recalcitrant beings and processes, the earth is potentially remakeable or actually remade, an artifact of external design. Though extreme in their sheer blankness, slated globes concretize a broader, typically modern transformative impulse. Their "makeability" implicitly pervades many conventional spatial representations used to inform and expedite transformative designs. Gathering and articulating the essential malleability of the world disclosed by machination, slated globes conjure the prospect of an earth so comprehensively reconstituted that "man," in Heidegger's gendered phrasing, "would everywhere and always encounter only himself."[37]

ENORDERING

Laying out an objectified, progressively pliant earth before an estranged and empowered human subject, the world pictures of machination were crucial to the formation and functioning of modernity's global empires and transformative projects. Yet drawing on revisionist accounts of Heidegger's later work (particularly that of Andrew J. Mitchell), I stress how machination is but one of two ontological disclosures at work in modernity for Heidegger. The other is *Gestell,* which Mitchell insists "is not to be identified with machination," for it is "essentially different from the order of objectivity and representation."[38]

Whereas machination involves detached subjects imposing their will on stable objects, *Gestell* entails the purposeless yet ceaseless circulation and switching about of fungible and flexible resources. Heidegger begins using the term after World War Two and it resonates with the postwar period's intensified commodification and globalization. In "The Question Concerning Technology," Heidegger explains that although the word *Gestell* usually designates an apparatus or structure such as a "bookrack" or "skeleton," he wields it in a "thoroughly unfamiliar" manner.[39] This new usage signifies "the way of revealing that holds sway in the essence of modern technology," which "demands that nature be orderable as standing-reserve" (that is, as flexible resources).[40] Despite being widely translated as "enframing," this falsifies the term's ontological import. To grasp *Gestell* "as some kind of framework or scaffolding thrown over the world," Mitchell explains, "is to persist in the belief that this incursion of the technological would be something that came to us from the outside, that it would remain somehow extrinsic to all that is."[41] As a translation, then, "enframing" obscures Heidegger's signal point that *Gestell* represents a transformation *within being*. Despite notions of framing being suggestive in relation to visual renditions of the planet, I therefore translate *Gestell* as "enordering." This is not intended to conjure up an image of subjects ordering the world, as under machination. Enordering is rather meant in the sense of "placing an order," someone "awaiting orders," or a product being "on order." It speaks to the restlessness of beings under this casting of being. People and things are perpetually on call to be summoned off to this or that destination, for this or that reason, always already stretched beyond themselves, entering circulation, and assuming new forms.

Enordering annuls the distance, objectivity, and malleability of machination. If previously the subject was placed "over and against" the object, implying an interval between them, Mitchell explains that "there is now a suffusion into that space and a smothering of the difference between subject and object in the general transformation into standing reserve."[42] Humans no longer presence as secluded Cartesian minds, but are drawn down into technological flows, included among bewitching commodities, and driven about as part of their frenzied mobility. Far from lording it over a petrified world, the subject too is "taken as standing-reserve."[43]

This does not mean that human subjects cross the threshold of representation to join the agglomeration of objects previously at their behest. Heidegger is clear that "there are no longer objects" under enordering.[44] Both subjects and objects are recast as something new: standing reserve, which, Mitchell notes, "does anything but stand."[45] Indeed, entities in the standing reserve are constantly marshaled or leveraged to facilitate new opportunities for operation; always being called toward the next assignment; ever mutating to execute new functions. "Standing," then, should indicate that beings are perpetually on standby, at the ready for renewed application. Contrast the stable and discrete object of machination. Entirely present and simultaneous with itself, the object bears consistent properties that the Baconian subject can pin down and work upon. The item of standing reserve offers no such solidity; it never coincides with itself. Instead, its being is dispersed through endless replacements and transformations in a chain of deferral that forecloses the possibility of the item being gathered up and set before a subject as an encapsulated entity.

This ontological instability is manifested in the standing reserve's replaceability, mutability, and placelessness. In *replaceability* not simply because ample substitutes stand ready for outmoded items and exhausted labor. A "piece of standing reserve," Heidegger explains, is "already imposed upon for replaceability" long before its actual replacement.[46] Its very being consists in replaceability: "The stock of items is already here replacing the item," Mitchell expands, "and this whole movement is written into the item itself."[47] Items of standing reserve are existentially defined by fungibility, then: their being is distributed across myriad absent replacements and equivalents.

In *mutability,* in that the standing reserve is ceaselessly changing. The object and item of standing reserve are both plastic, but their plasticity takes contrasting forms. Whereas subjects strive to remold the objectified world to realize determinate designs, the mutation of the standing reserve is endless that in it both goes on going on and has no goal beyond maintaining and increasing sociotechnical systems. As Heidegger remarks in his *Der Spiegel* interview, "everything functions," which "propels everything more and more toward further functioning."[48] The object's malleability is replaced by the standing reserve's endless flexibility and adaptability. In discussing a hydroelectric plant, Heidegger describes how the "energy concealed in nature is unlocked, what is unlocked is transformed, what is transformed is stored up, what is stored up is in turn distributed, and what is distributed is switched about ever anew."[49] For Hubert Dreyfus, these conversions presuppose that beings are "completely flexible, adaptable, optimizable" in ways that anticipate "digitalized information," which, in being sampled, scraped, transferred, encoded, and aggregated, is defined by its capacity to be "switched about ever anew."[50]

In *placelessness,* for if the standing reserve is replaceable and constantly available, then each item is always anywhere else, despite being here, and every other item is always here, despite being elsewhere. "Even when 'in' place," Mitchell explains, "the standing reserve is already tending 'toward' something else, arriving from somewhere else."[51] This placelessness implies a complete and closed—that is, global—space of exchange and circulation, what Heidegger calls the "circuit of orderability," around which the standing reserve switches about endlessly.[52] This global circuitry of instantaneous supply, mobility, and exchange, Mitchell emphasizes, "does not lead any where, it only ever feeds back into itself."[53] As such, global infrastructures materially instantiate enordering's inward-turning logic of continually optimized functionality without ultimate purpose.

ENORDERING EARTH

Global images pervade contemporary culture and locational media. Although initially this might suggest that the world is presencing as picture more completely than ever, my claim is that the transformation of global representation precipitated by digitization actually signals the waning of machination and waxing of enordering. I make this argument through a discussion of Google Earth, the most prominent digital figuration of the global to date. Although one might suppose Heidegger's thought to have little to say about geospatial technologies developed after his time, it is worth recalling his well-known remark that "the essence of technology is nothing technological," but consists instead in "a mode of revealing."[54] In line with this, by approaching Google Earth alongside Heidegger's thinking of enordering, I hope to mount a specifically ontological analysis of the application, attuned not just to its technological affordances but also to the basic disclosure of the world that they presuppose and articulate.

Developed in the late 1990s before being acquired by Google in 2004, the program presents a spheroid mosaic in which thousands of aerial and satellite photographs are layered onto a coordinated geode (the World Geodetic System 1984). In allowing users to view, rotate, reorient, and (in certain extensions) remap the globe, Google Earth appears to reproduce the distance, objectification, and malleability of machination. It would be perverse, therefore, to argue that Google Earth represents a clean break with the age of the world picture: to a degree, it still operates in a universe of detached visuality. Yet this is true only of aspects of the program. Its most distinct features—those which mark it out as belonging to a new, digital and distributed phase in the history of global representation—transgress machination's founding distinctions and disclose the earth in ways that approximate enordering's endless flexibility and fungibility. I begin by describing how Google Earth empties and disperses subjectivity through the represented world.

Three functions combine to diminish, if not annul, the difference between the viewing subject and objectified world that defined machination. First, the program's zoom invites users to transition rapidly among spatial scales, from the whole earth with which it opens to innumerable locales (Figure 4). If previously the subject saw the world from afar, the zoom induces users to span that distance, which is substituted for proximity. More radically, Vittoria Di Palma argues that the zoom does not simply span distances, but renders questions of size, space, and distance irrelevant by cycling through different "degrees of resolution" in ways that do "not necessarily have anything to do with physical displacement."[55] Jettisoning the gaze from "the anchoring dimensions of the human body," the zoom eschews intuitions of distance and hierarchies of scale, such that "the infinitely large and the infinitely small—the world and the atom, the planet and the point— are made comparable."[56] Whereas the detached subject of machination confronts an earth conceived as a vast objectified body, the zoom operates beyond near and far, large and small, echoing Heidegger's stress on the "distancelessness" of enordering. This creates what Di Palma calls the "fantasy of an intimate globe" in which both globality and locality are "present and immediately accessible simply by dragging or clicking the mouse."[57]

Second, Google Earth's diminution of distances accelerated with the integration of Google Street View in 2008. After dropping a dangling avatar into a photographed roadway, users transfer into Street View, where they navigate branching ground-level prospects captured by vehicle-mounted cameras. Viewers are drawn down to earth, moving from a satellite to an earthbound view. No longer a surface set against them, the world comes in encircling vistas. It might be countered that Google's roadway panoramas objectify people and places on a horizontal plane in much the same way that modern maps vertically conquer the world as picture, but this overlooks how the next feature blurs the very distinction between self and world.

Figure 4. Google Earth's zoom (Santiago). Map data: Google, SIO, NOAA, U.S. Navy, NGA, GEBCO, Landsat/Copernicus, Maxar Technologies, Data LDEO-Columbia, NSF, and IBCAO.

Third, Google Earth incorporates user-generated media. Users upload personal archives of photographs and videos,[58] which, linked to relevant locations, build a common, networked spatiality; geotag businesses and social ventures, which link to websites, photographs, reviews, and related locations; and create overlays, which map specific, often personal themes, as well as "stories" (multiform presentations combining maps, aerial and street views, videos, photographs, and text) that can be shared online. Even forums criticizing Google Earth can be expanded from placemarks affixed to the globe. In this way, Jason Farman explains, the program can "present user-generated content and dialog spatially on the very object that such content critiques."[59]

Together, these features indicate that in Google Earth human being is not defined by its detachment from the extant world, but dispersed and articulated through it. The earth becomes a dynamic texture in which the self is embedded and expressed. This indicates neither the objectification of the self nor subjectification of the world, for subject and object exist only in their difference. Instead, both self and world collapse into flexible, often searchable data, which, as Dreyfus suggested, can be read as embodying the standing reserve's restless mutability.

The subject fades into the standing reserve, then, in tandem with the onset of another disclosure of the earth. In many respects, Google Earth's representation of the earth reflects Heidegger's description of how enordering casts beings not as objects but items of standing reserve. At one level, the program facilitates the expansion and circulation of the standing reserve. Presenting an indexed, searchable, and navigable globe, it coordinates diverse sites to, from, and across which resources are summoned and switched about. At another, the digital globe itself embodies the move from object to standing reserve. Whereas the world picture of machination offers a stable surface, Google Earth presents a teeming mosaic of periodically refreshed satellite photographs in a continually honed interface.

Although Google Earth is readily construed as a slated globe for the digital age, inheriting and extending the world picture's malleability, its plasticity is of a different order. If subjects set out to transform the "makeable" world picture to realize determinate socio-spatial blueprints, under enordering beings and environments are perpetually altered and adapted to ensure uninterrupted service and facilitate unending growth, without an ultimate existential purpose. Constantly mutating through myriad piecemeal updates, modifications, and additions, Google Earth mirrors the standing reserve's restlessness and replaceability, in which beings are always already shadowed by their impending substitution. Timestamps underscore how satellite photographs and street panoramas await renewal from the moment they are uploaded; thousands of networked users thicken the terrestrial surface with their media; and occasionally geographies are physically rearranged to address Google's satellite gaze. Instead of pushing toward some final condition in modernist fashion, these changes expand and optimize technosocial systems, from the program itself to the economies it mediates.

In other respects, Google Earth's vision of being is more fraught and ambivalent than Heidegger's stark description of enordering might suggest, tempering two aspects of Heidegger's account in particular. First, Heidegger describes how beings revealed as standing reserve are constantly conscripted, allocated, and transformed to ensure endless, uninterrupted operation. Beings are "placed into application," which is "ordered in advance as a success," defined as "that type of consequence that itself remains assigned to the yielding of further consequences."[60] Circular, inward-turning functionality reigns. Google Earth, in contrast, is cluttered with anomalous sights, technical glitches, and ludic possibilities that have little imaginable technological or economic utility (save perhaps as curiosities in online attention economies). This comes forth in Kingsbury and Paul Jones III's vivid description of the program as "an uncertain orb spangled with vertiginous paranoia, frenzied navigation, jubilatory dissolution, and intoxicating giddiness."[61] Concerned to complicate the received critique of global images as exemplars of detachment and domination, they stress instances of errancy and anachronism, frenzy and play, breakdown and mystery that proliferate in the interstices of the geocoded world, including conspiracist sightings of black helicopters, glimpses of nudity, profanities mown into cornfields, mysterious tears in the global surface, and the joys of navigating a composite earth. If these things seem purposeless, it is not the purposelessness of the standing reserve, which is endless precisely because it is locked into a circular compulsion to optimize its own operation. Google Earth's oddities fall outside the imperative that beings should apply successfully and yield more successful applications without end. Far from ushering in total mobilization, then, enordering's global reach only illuminates regions of beings that elude subsumption into the standing reserve.

Second, anticipating globalization theorists of the 1990s, Heidegger emphasizes how "all distances in time and space are shrinking" into the "uniformly distanceless" with the acceleration of travel and proliferation of media.[62] No mere technological feat, this is ontologically preconditioned by enordering, under which beings show up as so available and replaceable that they are neither near nor far, never entirely here or there. That Google Earth, a geospatial application, has become so popular and pervasive troubles this emphasis on distancelessness. At one level, in making remote places navigable, the program collapses distances as Heidegger describes. At another, though, its success indicates that space and location not only persist as basic horizons of everyday life, but have become all the more important amid the frenzied circulation and replaceability of beings in the standing reserve. Capitalizing on the fact that many search queries contain geographical terms (thirty percent according to one technologist), Google organizes many results geographically, prompting users to transfer into its geospatial applications.[63] Including expandable media, which encode users' memories, Google Maps and Earth also thicken locations into places. Perhaps these dynamics interact in Google Earth, which both facilitates the atrophy of distances and switching about of resources *and* betrays an impulse to assert location, spatial orientation, and sites of memory against placeless globality.

CLASHING GLOBES

Midway through his fraught interview with *Der Spiegel* magazine in 1966, Heidegger described being "shocked when a short time ago I saw the pictures of the earth taken from the moon. We do not need atomic bombs at all—the uprooting of man is already here. All our relationships have become merely technical ones. It is no longer upon an earth that man lives today."[64] Equating existential estrangement with atomic devastation and fetishizing rootedness, these remarks exhibit Heidegger at his most mournful and absolute. This partly has to do with the interview's dynamic, with Heidegger attempting to impress the urgency of his thinking of planetary technicity on his often deadpan interlocutors. Moreover, as Lazier points out, he was responding not to the luscious "Blue Marble" and "Earthrise" images, but forbidding monochromes taken by Lunar Orbiter 1, in which earth appears farther off, dwarfed by a desolate moon. These, understandably, might have seemed "frightening in the extreme."[65]

Nonetheless, in reaching for photographs of the earth to concretize the existential uprooting wrought by technicity, Heidegger's somber remarks in this interview have set the parameters within which many subsequent writers have construed representations of the earth. Looking beyond this emphasis on the alienation wrought by planetary technicity, this essay has ventured a more expansive and multivalent Heideggerian approach to global representation, premised on the thought that images of the earth can be read as visions of being in its shifting historical modes. My analyses show how a handful of global representations distill and set forth the two divergent ontological determinations that, for Heidegger, undergird modern history. Establishing vertiginous distances between self and world, early modern world maps conjugate with Heidegger's description of how beings bifurcate into subjects and objects under machination. Presenting a global tabula rasa, slated globes crystallize the world's malleability in this casting of being. And in embedding networked users in a global mosaic, Google Earth collapses the distance between self and world and embodies the restlessness and replaceability of beings under enordering.

But these test cases also speak back to Heidegger's thinking of machination and enordering. Although early modern mapmakers invoked metaphors of elevation and externality to configure a transcendent new subject, these never quite put the self beyond earthly claims. Aspirant Apollos go the way of Icarus, towers teeter, crowds mob the stage. As for enordering, Heidegger described how it conditions a system of complete functionality, so encompassing and connected that space and distance evaporate. Yet Google Earth not only asserts the persistence of spatiality against distancelessness, but is peppered with oddities and glitches that confound utility. As an ontological vision, the program underscores how enordering, for all its totalizing propensities, will never subsume everything under placeless technicity.

■ ■ ■

In closing, I want to gesture toward the contemporary resonances of my discussion by pushing against another aspect of Heidegger's thinking: his account of the history of being, in which a series of disclosures of the world emerge, ground the unfolding of the epochs in which they appear, and then wane as another dispensation takes hold.[66] Although the possibility of creatively reappropriating past ontologies is ever-present, Heidegger narrates this history as a sequence of largely discrete stages. Mitchell and Dreyfus reproduce this periodizing impulse in extrapolating the distinction between machination and enordering from Heidegger's writings. Stressing how the two disclosures correspond to distinct epochs, they describe machination as "modern" and enordering "postmodern."[67] So much is in keeping with Heidegger. My analyses, however, prompt me to query the extent to which disclosures of being come in consolidated blocks. Mapping a global space of circulation (not least for trading Moluccan spices), Dutch cartography prefigures enordering's frenzied switching about of fungible stock. Further, although the world becomes picture in early modern mapmaking, it is grasped as a wholly makeable surface only centuries later, in slated globes, indicating that machination did not take hold evenly, all at once. And in allowing for detached viewing alongside other, more immersive vantage points, Google Earth lingers in the age of the world picture.

All of which leads me to think that machination and enordering are best imagined not as anything so neat as encapsulated periods but rather as discrepant yet enduring faces of modernity. This is not to diminish the difference between the two ontologies, but to acknowledge how they variously clash and overlap across modern history. Either might come to the fore under particular circumstances or recede for a period; that I have been able to present Dutch world maps and slated globes as paradigms of machination and Google Earth as exemplifying enordering suggests as much. Even so, neither machination nor enordering ever wins out over the other entirely. Far from mapping onto a single chronological break, the ontological fissure between them cuts jaggedly across diverse situations and stages of modernity.

This grating between contrary ontologies may be among the basic perplexities afflicting the current moment of climate doom loops and faltering geopowers. In salient discourses among mainstream environmental analysts and policymakers on how societies might redress climate heating, the emphasis on rendering global capitalism ecologically sustainable is increasingly accompanied by proposals to cool the earth's climate through geoengineering. These approaches are distilled, respectively, in *carbon offsetting*, "whereby quantified units of environmental harm . . . are traded or 'offset' for compensating units of environmental health at different places," and *solar radiation management,* which involves "injecting aerosols into the atmosphere to block incoming sunlight."[68] Establishing equivalences among incommensurable ecosocial processes, offsetting bespeaks a world in which the very materiality of beings and practices is negated across spectral doubles in remote times and places. Instead of seeking physically to manipulate resources and remake environments in line with machination, carbon offsetting substitutes otherwise constant processes for each other in a way that suggests the pervasive fungibility of enordering. And in venturing to modify the atmosphere, solar radiation management takes the earth as the pliant object of human design. Programmatically reconstituting the planetary environment in this way would represent the very essence of machination and apogee of the age of the world picture.

To me, the prominence of these strategies indicates that ecological policy and practice are pulled between discrepant visions of the planetary ecology they promise to rectify, visions that conjugate with the disclosures traced through this essay. Which other human practice depends so completely on the replaceability of beings established by enordering as carbon offsetting? Which other undertaking enacts the subject of machination's managerial attitude so faithfully as solar geoengineering? Far from sedimenting into distinct periods, these global ontologies play out jarringly in contemporary ecosocial practice, unfolding in increasingly extreme and concentrated forms.

DR SIMON FERDINAND (www.simonferdinand.com) is a postdoctoral researcher in Literary and Cultural Analysis at the University of Amsterdam. His work explores the politics and poetics of geographical representation, focusing particularly on cultural visions of the planetary environment. Recent publications include *Mapping Beyond Measure: Art, Cartography, and the Space of Global Modernity* (University of Nebraska Press, 2019) and the edited volumes *Heterotopia and Globalisation in the Twenty-First Century* (Routledge, 2020, with Irina Souch and Daan Wesselman) and *Other Globes: Past and Peripheral Imaginations of Globalization* (Palgrave, 2019, with Irene Villaescusa-Illán and Esther Peeren).

NOTES

1. This publication stems from the project "Untimely World Pictures: Confronting the Anthropocene Through Historical Representations of the Global Environment" (grant number VI.Veni.201C.048) of the Veni SGW research program, which is financed by the Dutch Research Council (NWO). Thanks to Michelle Niemann and two anonymous reviewers for their helpful commentary on the developing manuscript (any shortcomings are mine).

2. Despite seeming to address one and the same object, the words "earth," "world," "planet, and "globe" have divergent connotations and histories (see the introduction, written by myself, Irene Villaescusa-Illán, and Esther Peeren, to *Other Globes: Past and Peripheral Imaginations of Globalization* (Cham: Palgrave, 2019), 5–10). Lacking a neutral term for totality and wanting to avoid an overly rigid semantics, I refer alternately to "global representation," "images of the earth," and "the planet" in the knowledge that these formulations accentuate different aspects of what they describe. On the pervasiveness and inconspicuousness of global images, see Bronislaw Szerszynski and John Urry, "Visuality, Mobility, and the Cosmopolitan: Inhabiting the World from After," *The British Journal of Sociology* 57, no.1 (2006): 113–131.

3. Jennifer Wenzel, "Planet vs. Globe," *English Language Notes* 52, no. 1 (2014): 20. To give a prominent example of this critical strategy, Gayatri Chakravorty Spivak proposed "the planet to overwrite the globe." Whereas the safely controllable globe exists only "on our computers," Spivak sets up planetarity as a figure of "alterity" that is "best imagined from . . . precapitalist cultures"; *Death of a Discipline* (New York: Columbia University Press, 2003), 72, 101.

4. Christophe Bonneuil and Jean-Baptiste Fressoz, *The Shock of the Anthropocene* (London: Verso, 2017), 62.

5. Denis Cosgrove influentially argues that Western traditions of global imagining comprise a detached "Apollonian" visuality that has variously occasioned dreams of top-down power, reflection on earthly transience, and perceptions cosmic harmony; *Apollo's Eye: A Cartographic Genealogy of the Earth in the Western Imagination* (Baltimore: Johns Hopkins University Press, 2002). Although Cosgrove traces the Apollonian gaze back to ancient Greek culture, aspects of this visuality have been inculcated, imposed, or appropriated from around the world through colonialism.

6. Howard Caygill, "Heidegger and the Automatic Earth Image," *Philosophy Today,* 65, no. 2 (2021): 325–38; John Gilles, "Posed Spaces: Framing in the Age of the World Picture," in *The Rhetoric of the Frame: Essays on the Boundaries of the Artwork,* edited by Paul Duro, 24–43 (Cambridge: Cambridge University Press, 1996); Yuk Hui, "For a Planetary Thinking," *e-flux* 114 (2020), unpaginated; Adrian Ivakhiv, "The Age of the World Motion Picture: Cosmic Visions in the Post-Earthrise Era" in *The Changing World Religion Map,* ed. Stanley Brunn (Dordrecht: Springer, 2015), 129–44; W.J.T. Mitchell, "World Pictures: Globalization and Visual Culture," *Neohelicon* 34, no. 2 (2007): 49–59; Benjamin Lazier, "Earthrise; or, the Globalization of the World Picture," *The American Historical Review* 116, no .3 (2011): 602–630; Kelly Oliver, *Earth & World: Philosophy After the Apollo Missions* (New York: Columbia University Press, 2015); Sumathi Ramaswamy, *Terrestrial Lessons: The Conquest of*

the World as Globe (Chicago: Chicago University Press, 2010), xvii; Emilio Vavarella, "On Counter-Mapping and Media-Flânerie: Artistic Strategies in the Age of Google Earth, Google Maps, and Google Street View," in *Error, Ambiguity, and Creativity: A Multidisciplinary Reader,* edited by Sita Popat and Sarah Whatley, 137–66 (Cham: Palgrave, 2020), esp. 140.

7. For an excellent discussion of how Heidegger's reflections on the world picture have been taken up in work on images of the global environment, see Cory Austin Knudson, "Seeing the World: Visions of Being in the Anthropocene," *Environment, Space, Place* 12, no .1 (2020): 52–82.

8. Knudson, "Seeing the World," 62; Tim Ingold, "Globes and Spheres: The Topology of Environmentalism," in *Environmentalism: The View from Anthropology,* ed. Kay Milton (London: Routledge, 1993), 35.

9. As part of this unifying tendency, commentators have glossed over differences between Machenschaft and Gestell, which revisionist readings suggest name distinct ontologies. See for example Eliane Escoubas' claim that "Machenschaft says the same things as Gestell"; qtd. in Federico José Lagdameo, "From *Machenschaft* to *Ge-stell:* Heidegger's Critique of Modernity," *Filocracia* 1, no. 1 (2014), 4.

10. Thomas Sheehan, *Making Sense of Heidegger* (London: Rowman & Littlefield, 2015), 283.

11. Specifically, I am drawing on Federico José Lagdameo, who suggests that machination and enordering accord humans different roles with respect to other beings, as well as Hubert Dreyfus and Andrew J. Mitchell, who argue that machination and enordering name wholly distinct ontologies; Lagdameo, "From *Machenschaft* to *Ge-stell*": 1–23; Dreyfus,"15 of 26—Later Heidegger," *YouTube,* uploaded by Varuna, 30 November, 2014. https://www.youtube.com/watch?v=zbu _BVyPCuc&list=PLO1PGfOvgnmrqnTx_gHSZrfhCcXHkYFWG&index=15, 33:12, 27:26; Mitchell, *The Fourfold: Reading the Late Heidegger* (Evanston: Northwestern University Press, 2015). Somewhat earlier, Fredric Jameson also noted that Heidegger's thinking of machination "does not seem immediately reconcilable" with enordering, claiming that "in Heidegger there is not one modern break, but rather at least two"; *A Singular Modernity: Essay on the Ontology of the Present* (London: Verso, 2002), 58.

12. For a detailed account of how machination and enordering sit in the development of Heideggerian philosophy, see Mitchell, *Fourfold,* chapter 1.

13. On articulations of the global in Heideggerian philosophy, see for example Antonio Cerella and Louiza Odysseos, eds., *Heidegger and the Global Age* (London: Rowman and Littlefield, 2017.) On how global images relate to other aspects of Heidegger's thinking of modernity than I discuss here, see the works cited in n. 6.

14. Martin Heidegger, *Contributions to Philosophy (Of the Event),* trans. Richard Rojcewicz and Daniela Vallega-Neu (Bloomington: Indiana University Press, 2012), 98.

15. Martin Heidegger, "The Age of the World Picture," in *Off the Beaten Track,* trans. and ed. Julian Young and Kenneth Haynes (Cambridge: Cambridge University Press, 2002), 82.

16. Ibid, 67.

17. Ibid, 68.

18. Ibid, 68.
19. Ibid, 66.
20. Ibid, 66.
21. Martin Heidegger, *Nietzsche,* vol. 3, *The Will to Power as Knowledge and as Metaphysics,* edited by David Farrell Krell (San Francisco: HarperCollins, 1987), 175.
22. Heidegger, *Nietzsche,* 180.
23. Heidegger, "World Picture," 66.
24. Ibid, 71.
25. Ayesha Ramachandran, *The Worldmakers: Global Imagining in Early Modern Europe* (Chicago: Chicago University Press, 2015), 5.
26. David Harvey, *The Condition of Postmodernity: An Enquiry into the Origins of Cultural Change* (Oxford: Blackwell, 1989), 242.
27. Quoted in Denis Cosgrove, *Apollo's Eye,* 131.
28. Ibid, 2.
29. Gerhard Mercator, *Atlas or a geographicke description, of the regions, countries and kingdomes of the world, through Europe, Asia, Africa, & America,* trans. Henry Hexham (Amsterdam: Hondius and Johnson, 1636), unpaginated.
30. See Veronica della Dora, *The Mantle of the Earth: Genealogies of Geographical Metaphor* (Chicago: University of Chicago Press, 2021), 103.
31. Ibid, 103; Richard Butsch, "Crowds, Publics and Consumers: Representing English Theatre Audiences from the Globe to the OP Riots," *Journal of Participations: Audience and Reception Studies* 7, no. 1 (2010): 44.
32. Ramachandran, *Worldmakers,* 40.
33. Tim Ingold, "Globes and Spheres," 35.
34. Mercator, *Atlas,* unpaginated.
35. Ibid, unpaginated.
36. Mahshid Mayar, "What on earth! Slated Globes, School Geography and Imperial Pedagogy," *European Journal of American Studies* 15, no. 2 (2020): 1–19.
37. Martin Heidegger, "The Question Concerning Technology," in *Basic Writings,* ed. David Farrell Krell, trans. William Loveitt, 2nd. ed., (New York: Harper Collins, 1993,) 332.
38. Mitchell, *Fourfold,* 37.
39. Heidegger, "Question Concerning Technology," 325.
40. Ibid, 325, 328.
41. Mitchell, *Fourfold,* 50.
42. Ibid, 37.
43. Heidegger, "Question Concerning Technology," 332.
44. Quoted in Mitchell, *Fourfold,* 37.
45. Ibid, 48.
46. Martin Heidegger, "Positionality," in *Bremen and Freiburg Lectures: Insight Into That Which Is and Basic Principles of Thinking,* trans. Andrew J. Mitchell (Bloomington: Indiana University Press, 2012), 35.
47. Mitchell, *Fourfold,* 59.
48. Martin Heidegger, "'Only a God Can Save Us': The Spiegel Interview," in *Heidegger: The Man and the Thinker,* ed. Thomas Sheehan, trans. William J. Richardson (Chicago: Precedent, 1981), 56.

49. Heidegger, "Question Concerning Technology," 322.
50. Hubert Dreyfus, "15 of 26—Later Heidegger—Hubert Dreyfus Lecture," *YouTube,* uploaded by Varuna, 30 November, 2014. https://www.youtube.com/watch?v=zbu _BVyPCuc&list=PLO1PGfOvgnmrqnTx_gHSZrfhCcXHkYFWG&index=15, 33:12, 27:26.
51. Ibid, 48.
52. Heidegger, "Positionality," 31.
53. Mitchell, *Fourfold,* 52.
54. Heidegger, "Question Concerning Technology," 340, 319.
55. Vittoria Di Palma, "Zoom: Google Earth and Global Intimacy," in *Intimate Metropolis,* ed. Vittoria Di Palma, Diana Periton, and Marina Lathouri (London: Routledge, 2008), 260.
56. Ibid, 257.
57. Ibid, 263, 264.
58. Google selects media first uploaded to Google Maps to appear on Google Earth too.
59. Jason Farman, "Mapping the Digital Empire: Google Earth and the Process of Post-modern Cartography," *New Media and Society* 12, no. 6 (2010): 869.
60. Heidegger, "Positionality," 25.
61. Paul Kingsbury and John Paul Jones III, "Water Benjamin's Dionysian Adventures on Google Earth," *Geoforum* 40 (2009): 503.
62. Martin Heidegger, "The Point of Reference," in *Bremen and Freiburg Lectures,* 3, 4.
63. Ed Parsons, quoted in Jerry Brotton, *A History of the World in Twelve Maps* (London: Allen Lane, 2012), 429.
64. Heidegger, "Only a God," 56.
65. Lazier, "Earthrise," 610.
66. On this conception of history, see Philip Tonner, "Epoch: Heidegger and the Happening of History," *Minerva—An Open Access Journal of Philosophy* 19 (2015): 132–50.
67. Mitchell, *Fourfold,* 25.
68. Sian Sullivan, "What's Ontology got to do with it? On nature and knowledge in a political ecology of the 'green economy'," *Journal of Political Ecology* 24 (2017): 230; Holly Jean Buck, *After Geoengineering: Climate Tragedy, Repair, and Restoration* (London: Verso, 2019), 2.

Sonic Histories

Reckoning with Race through Campus Soundscapes[1]

TYLER KINNEAR, ROBERT HUNT FERGUSON,
AND JESSICA M. HAYDEN

Abstract

The sounds of the college campus raise important questions of participation, identity, privilege, disability, and marginalization. During the 2019–2020 academic year, three university instructors from distinct disciplines (music, history, and political science) and a student research assistant (history) used sound as a method for inquiring into contested and erased sites on the campus of Western Carolina University, a regional comprehensive university located in the southeastern United States. The project came to be called Sonic Histories. Paid student volunteers were led on a soundwalk and completed three online questionnaires that engaged questions of race and belonging on campus. This study presents findings on how students experience and interpret contested and erased sites through sounds heard and imagined. Sonic Histories explores two central questions. Historically, whose voices have been included and whose have been excluded on college campuses? How can sound promote awareness of racialized spaces and, in turn, achieve social engagement? The authors challenge the triumphant narrative of campus histories, which highlights racial reconciliation and progress while eliding the ways predominantly white campuses still exclude minorities. By re-centering minority voices in campus spaces, the authors explore the systemic exclusion of minorities that has occurred on college campuses across the country. At a time when places of higher education are refining and developing their commitment to diversity and inclusivity— while assessing their past in honest ways—the Sonic Histories project builds upon ongoing initiatives to position the college campus as a scholarly community that lives up to its democratic ideals of inclusion.

INTRODUCTION

"I've never thought about history in the context of sound. I've always visualized it and I never really thought about what it sounded like. It really put a new perspective on history."

—Student comment following a Sonic Histories soundwalk

Across America, universities whose histories are closely intertwined with slavery, white supremacy, and Jim Crow have pursued various measures of reconciliation. From the University of Alabama to Michigan State University, and Columbia University to the University of North Carolina at Chapel Hill, campus administrations are racing to rename buildings that, for decades, have honored slaveholders or segregationists. Yet, remnants of painful pasts still persist on campus landscapes, confounding administrators and galvanizing students and faculty. Monuments and building names serve as reminders to many students and employees that campuses have always been spaces where "belonging" is tenuous.

Soundwalking has become a popular exercise in higher education—and other areas—for exploring social issues. The premise is relatively straightforward: conduct a silent walk (alone or with a group, improvised or preplanned), giving attention to the sounds in one's immediate environment and one's response/reaction to those sounds.[2] In this way, soundwalking is not only about focused listening but also about resensitizing one's self to the environment. John Levack Drever observes, "one of the underpinning goals of soundwalking is about circumnavigating habituation, in a process of de-sensitization and consequently re-sensitization, in order to catch a glimpse (*un coup d'oreille*) of the 'invisible, silent and unspoken' of the everyday."[3] Arguably, conducting a soundwalk—and other forms of direct engagement with soundscapes—can lead to both immediate and long-term recalibrations of inclusion, equity, and cultural sustainability. The authors of this project adapted the soundwalk model and in 2019 launched a project called Sonic Histories on the campus of Western Carolina University (WCU).

The Sonic Histories project is inextricable from the historical moment in which it was born. In 2016, college campuses across the United States were flashpoints for the often-contentious debates over free speech, racial equality, and a hotly contested presidential election. Students expressed their beliefs, anxieties, and misgivings in classrooms, dorm rooms, student unions, and on social media. As students picked sides or looked on from the sidelines, tensions mounted. WCU was no different in this regard. In response to a campus Black Lives Matter (BLM) rally in 2016, one student reacted on Yik Yak (a social media platform): "Nothing is being achieved by you protesting here, and I'm sick of hearing about something that isn't even an issue."[4]

Space and sound were integral to campus communities' experiences of moments like this one. Notice how the space of the BLM protest, which took place at the Catafount—a central location on campus—intersects with the sounds of protestors' greivances, which the student claimed to be "sick of hearing about." In fact, at this particular protest, sound was marshalled in strategic ways by both the protesters and counter-protesters. Supporters of BLM chose to place tape over their mouths in silent protest. Students who opposed BLM often voiced their disagreement as they walked through the protest. In at least one incident, a student spat on another student protester. Sonic Histories, motivated by moments like the one above, sought to map the intersection of sonic and physical spaces on campus and their impact on the emotional and somatic experiences of students. This project aims to uncover how sound relates to belonging on campus. Moreover, Sonic Histories challenges WCU's triumphant narrative of progress by curating a lesson which gave students the time and space to actively listen to the sounds of inclusion and exclusion on their own campus.

Not long after a series of racially charged events transpired at WCU in 2016 and 2017, a campus working group concluded that the university was not doing enough to promote diversity and equality. As a result, the university administration asked several faculty and staff from various disciplines to create "diversity modules" to be taught in University Experience (USI) courses. These courses are required of all first-year students at WCU to socialize them to college life. As a result of this request, five diversity modules were created, including a sound-walk that was developed by the authors of this article. With the support of the director of First-Year Experience at WCU, the authors were able to develop Sonic Histories and get initial feedback from students and instructors. The overall project examines historic and present exclusion as it relates to race, class, gender, and disability. However, this specific research focuses exclusively on race as a mode of analysis.

During the 2019–2020 academic year, the authors used sound as a method for inquiring into contested and erased sites on the campus of WCU, a regional comprehensive university located in the southeastern United States. Fifty-seven voluntary students were led on a soundwalk and completed three online questionnaires that engaged questions of race and belonging on campus. The authors adopted the traditional soundwalk model, established by composer and acoustic ecologist Hildegard Westerkamp and the Vancouver Soundwalk Collective: introduction, walk, and open discussion.[5] During the Sonic Histories introduction, a trained student soundwalk leader explained logistics, distributed portfolios, and asked some larger questions to encourage participants to think critically about history, listening, and identity (ten minutes). Each walk consisted of between ten and fifteen participants, with a total of six walks conducted between November 5, 2019 and February 19, 2020. The walk itself (fifty minutes) led participants to seven historical sites on campus, in order: the Alumni (bell) Tower, the Killian Annex (site of the former Cherokee mound), Breese Gymnasium, Joyner Plaza, Robertson Residence Hall (site of the former Mount Zion African Methodist Episcopal Zion Church), McKee Building, and the Catafount (a fountain area used for social gatherings, cultural events, and protests) (see Figure 1). The walk was followed by fifteen minutes of open discussion; the discussion was recorded and transcribed for research purposes. At each site, participants viewed a portfolio of documents from the WCU Special Collections that encouraged reflection on the erased/contested sites under consideration, with specific attention to race, class, gender, (dis)ability, and belonging on campus.[6] In addition to the soundwalk, students completed pre-, post- and follow-up surveys, which were administered online using Qualtrics. The follow-up survey was distributed two weeks after each walk. Forty-three participants fulfilled all three surveys. In total, student participants committed two hours, receiving $55 compensation for their time and contributions.

Sonic Histories refines the model of soundwalking by focusing on how racial and ethnic minorities have been excluded from public spaces in history. During the soundwalks, students were encouraged to listen to stories of racial and ethnic exclusion and conflict that have occurred

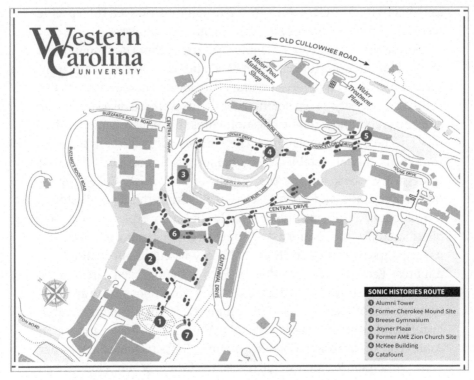

Figure 1. Sonic Histories Soundwalk Route. Image: Maura Soler Casademont.

in their lived space, while also listening to the sounds that currently exist in that space. In doing so, Sonic Histories invited participants to be both present and honest with a given soundscape, and this includes being aware and self-critical of one's own biases and privileges. In the post-walk survey, students reported that the soundwalk was an active, positive, and thought-provoking experience that elicited emotional reactions in many participants.

SOUNDWALKING: ORIGINS AND DIRECTIONS

Soundscapes play a pivotal role in understanding how minority voices have been historically and politically silenced. As Jennifer Lynn Stoever has argued, "reconsidering racialization as a sonic practice allows for a deeper understanding of why both race and racism persist."[7] Soundscapes are political spaces in which cultural sounds deliver important information. Cultural sounds not only preserve heritage and identity but also inform us of what matters to those who define—or even control—a given space.[8] Soundwalking can be an important step in the process of understanding which voices are audible, inaudible, dominant, suppressed, preserved, and lost.

The genesis of soundwalking began with the work of the World Soundscape Project (WSP) in the 1970s, a research team based in Vancouver, Canada. With the WSP, soundwalking was often the initial step in studying a soundscape. These walks were primarily improvised and were recorded for research purposes aimed at documenting changes in sonic environments and raising awareness to growing noise pollution.[9] Since the foundational work of the WSP, interest in soundwalking has grown exponentially in both academic and artistic areas. Applications can be seen in cultural ethnography, education, geography, sonic art, and urban planning, among other areas.[10] Sonic Histories builds on the original concept of soundwalking by inviting participants to observe sounds in their immediate environment and to reflect on what those sounds tell them about a place and about themselves. However, Sonic Histories encourages participants to attend to silenced voices, whereas the WSP focused on distinct human-associated sounds in a given soundscape (e.g., a belltower or a steam clock), issues of noise pollution, and/or the value of nature.

One danger of soundwalking is that it can take on qualities of sonic voyeurism; that is, the promise of intimacy when observing everyday sounds.[11] Combined with the Eurocentricity of the WSP's research subjects (i.e., documenting white colonial voices over those of minority groups), artists are increasingly engaging mobile listening with critical awareness towards sound, space, and self.[12] This is demonstrated by the use of decolonized and anti-racist walking practices in North America. For example, Camille Turner uses her Miss Canadiana persona to act as a tour guide of black histories in Toronto's Grange neighborhood. Turner and others are using walking as a method for exposing subjugated knowledge of black and/or indigenous histories and to give agency to marginalized groups.[13] Additionally, scholars are applying decolonizing methods across media and on-site and also raising awareness to the ethics of listening to and composing with culturally sensitive soundscapes.[14]

In the wake of social movements sweeping across the United States, Sonic Histories applies soundwalking to one of the most distinctive and socially charged spaces: the university campus. Other recent sound-walk projects that explore politicized spaces included Amanda Black and Andrea Bohlman's engagement with the "Silent Sam" Confederate soldier monument on the campus of the University of North Carolina at Chapel Hill and Georgios Varoutsos's work with the Peace Wall Belfast in Belfast, a series of physical barriers that separate Protestant/Loyalist neighborhoods and Catholic/Nationalist neighborhoods.[15] Sonic Histories departs from these projects in two ways. First, Sonic Histories charted a route around several contested sites on campus. Although Black and Bohlman's and Varoutsos's soundwalks present multiple stops, the two projects give particular attention to one contested space, a monument and a section of a wall, respectively. Consideration of several contested sites is arguably an advantage of Sonic Histories, as one can observe the different reactions among participants at different sites. Sonic Histories also fills a gap in previous soundwalk projects by applying both qualitative and quantitative research methods.[16] This approach helps us better understand how active listening can promote self-reflection and critical discussion around contemporary social issues.

CAMPUS AND THE TRIUMPHANT HISTORICAL NARRATIVE: THE CASE OF WESTERN CAROLINA UNIVERSITY

While flagship universities founded before the Civil War make national headlines with their approaches to reconciling troubled pasts, smaller universities' efforts often go relatively unnoticed beyond local news outlets. WCU has few obvious visual indicators of its complicated past with the Cherokee and African Americans. This is quite unlike many older southeastern universities. The Confederate soldier monument, that for over one hundred years guarded the entrance to the University of North Carolina (UNC), served as a constant reminder of the university's racist, sexist, and violent past.[17] While students, faculty, staff, and community activists at UNC pointed to the semiotic importance of "Silent Sam" and used the space around the monument for protests meant to push for a more inclusive, antiracist campus, WCU has no obvious contested spaces where historical and present struggles over belonging have coalesced. Yet, the contested history is present at WCU, lurking just below the surface.

The land on which WCU now resides was once a thriving Cherokee town.[18] WCU was founded in 1889, only twenty-five miles from the Qualla Boundary, the federally recognized home of the Eastern Band of the Cherokee Indian (EBCI). The university's relationship with the EBCI has sometimes been fraught. As recent research by historian Robert Lee and others has demonstrated, at least fifty-two land-grant universities were created due to the forced cessation of Native land. "The Morrill Act," argues Lee, "worked by turning land expropriated from tribal nations into seed money for higher education."[19] That research underscores and further confirms the plundering of Native American wealth and culture by United States' institutions. Public universities, even those not founded as land-grant institutions, have not fully confronted how their pasts intersect with the colonial conquest of Native American communities. Some of the earliest universities in the country, such as UNC, benefited directly from treaties, often illegal, that ceded indigenous land. When UNC was founded in 1789, it was "awarded thousands of acres of western lands by state legislators."[20] According to recent research, UNC survived the many financial upheavals of the 1800s by selling Cherokee and Chicaksaw land.[21]

Recent archeological research at WCU has uncovered a community that may have once been at the center of American Indian commerce and cultural activities. Until the 1950s, a ceremonial mound sat near the middle of campus. The mound was central to the Cherokee village in Cullowhee until the mid-17th century. Standing approximately 20-feet high, the original earthen mound was the base of the council house and the focal point of the community. The mound was one of numerous signs of Cherokee settlement in the area dating to approximately 500 years before European settlers. In 1956, however, the university bulldozed the mound to make way for a mixed-use office and classroom building. An article in the local newspaper encouraged readers to visit the site "for one last souvenir."[22]

In 2018, WCU student Todd Martin produced an eight-feet high iron sculpture entitled *Wi*, which the university installed near the former site

Figure 2. Martin (right), in conversation with Richard Sneed, Principal Chief of the Eastern Band of Cherokee. Photo: Randall Holcombe, "Eastern Band of Cherokee's ties to WCU landscape commemorated with unveiling of 'wi' sculpture," *WCU Stories* (September 24, 2018), https://www.wcu.edu/stories/posts/News/2018/09/eastern-band-of-cherokees-ties-to-wcu-landscape-commemorated-with-unveiling-of-wi-sculpture/index.aspx. Photo courtesy of WCU Communications & Marketing.

of the mound (see Figure 2). Martin took inspiration from the Cherokee language and syllabary. "Wi" translates in Cherokee as "the place" and is the root of the town name "Cullowhee." The installation was supported by the EBCI. Members of the tribe, including the principal chief, attended its unveiling. A small plaque acknowledges the existence of the Cherokee village and the previous presence of the mound. However, there is no mention nor historical context for the vandalization of the mound and the plaque utilizes the slippery passive voice to tell readers that the mound "was razed" without assigning a subject or acknowledging that the university participated in the removal of Cherokee history. The absence of explicit acknowledgement sharply juxtaposes active attempts at reconciliation with symbolic measures. While *Wi* was a student-created sculpture with the support of the WCU administration and local Cherokee leaders, does it help reconcile a fraught history or perpetuate a triumphant narrative of amelorization through memorialization?

The Sonic Histories project rejects the triumphant narrative of unmitigated American progress. Historian Jacquelyn Dowd Hall argues that movements for progressive change—particularly the Civil Rights Movement—has been "distorted and reified" in ways that ensures a bowdlerized version is enshrined in a "triumphal moment in a larger American progress narrative" that undermines the actual gravitas and radicalism of the movement.[23] Like Hall demonstrated with the Civil Rights Movement, Sonic Histories wants to make campus history "harder to celebrate as a natural progression of American values. Harder to celebrate as a satisfying morality tale. Most of all, harder to simplify, appropriate, and contain."[24] As faculty, we are cognizant of the fact that many diversity and inclusion efforts and learning activities at universities and elsewhere often frame the Civil Rights Movement using a triumphant narrative. The narrative often goes like this: that historical discrimination against racial minorities is a sad fact, but the university to which you belong has been consistently progressive relative to others at the time. These messages tend to be positive and uplifting—that while there is still work to do, we have always risen to the challenge. This triumphant narrative underestimates the oppression of racial minorities that occurred in the past and present.

The authors argue that the triumphant narrative ignores the continued effects of systemic racism and disengages students from their role in institutionalized racism. With this in mind, the authors chose an approach to a research module that required students to not only learn about racism that has occurred in their lived environment, but to be mindful of exclusion and inclusion of the past and present. As one student observed in the post-walk discussion following the soundwalk, "[W]hen I walk around Western [WCU], I feel a very positive, secure space. But we've taken and we've built something positive out of negative situations. And so is it positive or is it a false positive that we create in our heads? And a lot of people don't know about the history of these places."

Increasingly, WCU seems to be listening to its student body when it demands action. Students have recently led the charge to call for a zero-tolerance policy toward students who express racist views. After two separate social media videos were posted of students using racial slurs in September 2020, students across campus, including the Black Student Union, called for the immediate dismissal of the students in the videos for violating university community standards. After initially refusing to discuss potential discipline, within a week of concerted student demands, the administration announced that the students were no longer enrolled at WCU. Additionally, students have requested and received programs that more accurately reflect the entirety of the student body. As a result, WCU recently inaugurated programs in Latinx and Global Black Studies. Sonic Histories also grew out of campus initiatives to achieve measurable change and was inspired by the momentum of WCU's students who have consistently demanded the university live up to its stated core values. Additionally, Sonic Histories has been financially supported by our university through competitive grants and publicly supported by various administrators. It is our hope that the support WCU has shown for the soundwalks is indicative of the willingness the administration has to honestly assess its past and institute meaningful change in the present.

The authors chose campus sites that highlighted to participants the concealed nature of exclusion. Throughout the soundwalks, leaders asked participants to listen to their surroundings. During the debrief, however, one essential discussion topic was to think about the sounds and voices that have been historically silenced on campus. For example, WCU's history with racial integration is complicated. Typically, WCU has presented two examples to demonstrate that the university's approach to enrolling African American students into a previously all-white public institution was seamless and even progressive. In 1957, Lavern Hamlin enrolled in courses at WCU (then Western Carolina College) to complete her degree in post-secondary education. In doing so, she integrated WCU by becoming one of the first African American students at a previously all-white public college in North Carolina. By Hamlin's own recollection, her time at WCU was welcoming and productive. In 2019, a residential hall on campus was named in her honor. In 1964, Henry Logan became the first African American athlete to enroll in and play basketball for a predominately white institution in North Carolina. Logan went on to play professionally after shattering most of WCU's basketball records. While Hamlin's and Logan's presence on campus was notable, the triumphant narrative of a progressive small southern college graciously opening its doors to African Americans before its peers elides a more nuanced story.[25] Hamlin only attended WCU for three months during the summer of 1957 before finishing her degree and graduating. Logan left WCU, by some accounts, functionally illiterate after spending four years on campus.[26]

The WCU faculty did not include an African American instructor until 1974. In that year, the History Department hired Henry Lewis Suggs, a PhD candidate from the University of Virginia, to teach United States History and The History of Black America. Suggs would complete his PhD in 1976 and go on to an illustrious career as an academic, with appointments at Howard University, Clemson University, Harvard University, and North Carolina Central University. Suggs' short time at WCU, however, was not without incident. In 1976, a campus fraternity took out an advertisement in the student newspaper celebrating "eleven years of brotherhood" at WCU. The advertisement depicted Robert E. Lee, the Confederate battle flag, and fraternity members dressed in Confederate regalia. Suggs wrote an open letter to the fraternity in the campus newspaper asking them to think about the racist and insensitive implications of their advertisement and pointing out that African Americans were not welcome in the fraternity. Suggs received a phone call from the fraternity after the letter was published. The student on the other end sounded receptive to meeting with Dr. Suggs to discuss the issue. Several minutes later, however, the phone rang again. "We changed our minds," said the voice, and the call ended.[27] Suggs was not surprised nor perturbed. Several months before this, he had arrived to his campus office in the McKee Building to find the glass in his door broken, his belongings vandalized, and the words "Mafia Nigger" spray painted on a wall.[28]

As historian Mark M. Smith has pointed out, social historians are more concerned with the meanings that people in the past assigned to their auditory experiences than with attempting to recreate the sounds of the past.[29] This begs questions that Sonic Histories poses to students at the site of Suggs' former office in the McKee Building: What does racism sound like? Is it the sound of glass breaking? The frantic click-clacking of a spray paint can and the menacing hiss that follows as the perpetrator painted the epithet on Dr. Suggs' wall? We remind our students that, not long after this incident, Dr. Suggs left WCU for an appointment at Howard University. Not only was WCU late to hire an African American faculty member, but when he arrived, he encountered a hostile environment. Suggs' experience reveals that the long history of integration at WCU is not a triumphant tale of institutional progress, but a much more complex past that reflects the historic and present experiences of minorities on campus.

STUDENT PROFILES AND RECEPTIONS

The triumphant narrative typically begins and ends with a heroic act—a progressive policy, or the first of a demographic to come to campus—and skips the prologue of the institutional racism occurring before it, as well as the epilogue of the (sometimes negative) outcomes of the policy or acceptance of an individual. Physically, this triumphant narrative tends to manifest as decontextualized sculptures and plaques, lofty mission statements, or boilerplate language in syllabi. A deeper acknowledgment of and reconciliation with these histories is necessary for meaningful change. The above examples demonstrate how our university uses this narrative, but WCU is by no means the only institution. The triumphant narrative is utilized by universities and other long-standing institutions across the nation. It serves largely to absolve the current inhabitants of a given space from any complicity in the historical or existing structure of institutionalized racism that defines these spaces. This is particularly true for temporary, residential students on a college campus, who are likely unaware of—and feel no responsibility for—acts and policies of racism that occurred before their residency.

Student Profile

WCU is a state university in the UNC system which primarily serves a rural region in the Appalachian mountains. WCU is in a particularly rural location for a university of its size. It is positioned on 682 acres serving over 12,000 students, while the county in which WCU sits has a population of a little over 40,000. Currently, about 80% of WCU undergraduate students are white and over 40% are first generation college students.[30]

Of the 109 students who took the soundwalk pre-survey, a vast majority are white undergraduate students who were 22 years-old or younger at the time of the soundwalk. About 13% of respondents identify as racial or ethnic minorities including African American, Latinx, Asian, and American Indian. In addition to other basic demographic questions, participants were also asked about their listening habits, including how often they listen actively and how often they wear earbuds around campus. Participants were also asked about racial perceptions, including the identification of groups with which they felt a linked fate,[31] as well as identification of which groups are most discriminated against in the United States. The post-walk survey emphasized the experience of campus through sound, whereas the pre-walk survey sought to better understand student experiences of history, listening, and race. This emphasis on campus soundscapes in the post-walk survey can be seen in such questions that explored how the student interacted with soundscapes on the walk and what types of emotions were activated by the sounds of the sites visited on the soundwalk.

Student Receptions

Many college educators have experienced coldness or even hostility from students when teaching diversity, inclusion, or anti-racism due to the negative feelings of guilt and defensiveness on the part of white students, and feelings of being formally "othered" during lessons from racial minority students.[32] It is imperative that students find these types of lessons approachable, and it is heartening that the soundwalk in this study was well received by participants who are mostly undergraduate students at a majority-white, rural institution. A vast majority of our participants reported positive feelings toward the soundwalk experience, and expressed being more familiar with WCU's history after the soundwalk (56% report feeling very familiar after the soundwalk compared to 6% before). Many students reported having enjoyed learning about history through listening and sound. Thirty out of the 57 respondents to the post-walk survey reported enthusiastic or fully-positive feelings toward the soundwalk. These include responses ranging from "enlightening" and "very informative" to "fun" and "all students" should complete this activity. Also, in the follow-up survey, 27 respondents noted that they have become more actively mindful of sounds on campus, or as one student put it, "I try to be more conscious of the sounds around me and take in each and every one of them."

Another student stated, "I tend to think of the sound walk more than what I thought I would. The sound walk has helped with thinking about the sounds I'm experiencing around me."

Each of these statements are representative of what is a broad positive reception from student participants. Despite the fact that more students reported negative feelings about WCU's campus after the soundwalk than before, the soundwalk itself elicited positive feelings—often of empowerment through new knowledge. On the whole, students reported that the activity was eye-opening or informative, either in the discussion sessions following the actual soundwalk or in the post-walk survey. Moreover, each participant (n=57/57) reported a desire to know more about one or more of the sites' histories.

Even two weeks later, in the follow-up survey, many respondents (n=27/43) noted that they became more actively mindful of sounds on campus, or as one student put it, "I try to be more conscious of the sounds around me and take in each and every one of them." Another student stated that they used to "block everything out but now I listen to what is happening around me." Some students changed their routes to classes to alter their sonic surroundings, or to avoid places dominated by human sounds. Others reported walking around without headphones more often, or choosing to only keep one earbud in so as to "appreciate that our campus still contains organic sounds." The lasting impact of the soundwalk did not escape our participants. One student stated, "I tend to think of the sound walk more than what I thought I would. But the sound walk has helped with thinking about the sounds I'm experiencing around me."

The authors do find some more critical responses (n=5), including that it was too focused on negative historical events, that the silence required by the soundwalk inhibited discussion and learning, and that there was too much focus on racism. These comments, taken together, indicate that future soundwalks might frame the activity as one that addresses issues of racism so that participants are not surprised by the historical perspective of the soundwalk. However, the tone of the walk is in keeping with our goal of dispelling the triumphant narrative, and so a focus on negative historical events is imperative to the activity.

Figure 3 presents a word cloud as a visualization of the participants' responses to questions about the emotional impact the student experi-

Figure 3. Word Cloud of Student Survey Responses to Questions Regarding the Impact of the Soundwalk.

enced during the soundwalk, what they would like to say about the sites visited, as well as whether that emotional impact had a lasting effect and whether since the soundwalk (in the follow-up survey) students have changed the way they interact with sounds on campus. As demonstrated in this figure, the most common words students used in these answers (n=5,557 words) were "campus", "experience", "history", "soundwalk", and "think", demonstrating students' efforts to think about sounds, and their experience, on campus now more often than before the soundwalk.

While positively influencing students' active, mindful listening on campus has inherent value, an exploration of some of the less common words begins to indicate how this change has concurrently helped students who participate in this activity become more cognizant of new and old sounds on campus. Words like "learn", "felt", "surprised", "Cherokee", "African" [American], and "racism" are all indications of how this soundwalk helps students observe those included and excluded from the university's soundscape. The following section explores how the authors used student responses to evaluate whether the soundwalk helped encourage students to challenge the triumphant narrative and their role in it.

STUDENT REACTIONS TO SOUNDWALK SITES

Each university in the United States has been affected by racism in some way. That is why it is vital that an activity that broaches the discussion of racial and ethnic diversity and inclusion at a university challenges a triumphant narrative, and fosters introspection about the role individuals play in perpetuating racist policies. While students voiced that the soundwalk was enjoyable and that it helped them become more mindful listeners, it is more important that it also accomplishes its pedagogical goal of challenging racist policies perpetuated by the triumphant narrative and acknowledging patterns of exclusion both past and present. Consistently, the authors find that, after the soundwalk, many students questioned our university's policies toward exclusion of racial minorities and their role in the perpetuation of these policies. This next section details these findings by describing student responses to three diverse sites. These sites exhibit discrimination against both African Americans and Cherokee as well as feature racial conflict that occurred in the more distant past as well as events that occured quite recently. In order, these are the Mount Zion African Methodist Episcopal Zion Church (AME Zion Church), which was moved for the construction of a new dormitory; the Cherokee mound, which was razed to make room for new campus construction; and the Catafount, WCU's water feature named for its mascot the Catamount, which is a campus hub for social and political gatherings that has recently been the site of Black Lives Matter protests and counter-protests.

Former AME Zion Church Site

To demonstrate the soundscapes of exclusion on WCU's campus, our soundwalk brings students to the former site of the AME Zion Church. Built in 1897 by 11 African Americans who were slaves or descendants of slaves, the original site was on the hill where a dormitory (Robertson Hall) now stands (Figure 4). As described in a May 29, 1929 letter

Figure 4. AME Zion Church members circa 1920s, # HL_MSS03–09_27, Special Collections, Hunter Library, Western Carolina University.

from WCU President H. T. Hunter to North Carolina Attorney General Dennis G. Brummitt, the planned relocation of the church and 76 graves was framed as a potential legal issue, not for the university or the state but for the the church members (Figure 5). The land where the original church was located was sold later that year to the university for $4,200 ($1,000 of which paid for the relocation of 76 graves). The AME Zion Church and graveyard are now located one half mile east of the former site (Figure 6).

Many students were moved by the mistreatment of the members of this church by the former WCU community, with some noting explicitly that it was "underlying racism" driving the choices. Students report feeling uncomfortable, angry, and sad at the mistreatment of the church members. One respondent went a step further saying that it was "we" who took things from the church, rather than an abstract

May 29, 1929.

Hon. Dennis G. Brummitt, Atty. Gen.
Raleigh, North Carolina.

Re: Removal of Bodies from Graves

Dear Sir:

You will recall that the Legislature of 1921, I
believe, or possibly 1923, authorized Cullowhee State Normal
to condemn cemeteries and to remove the bodies.

Some time ago we purchased the property of the
negro church adjacent to our campus. There are 76 graves
on the lot, which we want to use at once for a new dormitory
site. We are ready to have the graves removed. A contract
has been entered into by which the trustees of the negro
church will actually have charge of the removal of the bodies.

The negroes are afraid of doing something which will
involve them in a lawsuit. I wish you would write me fully
what will be the legal requirements in the removal of the bodies. Will we have to get the consent of the nearest relative,
for instance? We have a written contract with the trustees
of the church to remove the bodies to a new site purchased
by the negro church. Will we have to give notice of intention to remove the bodies in a newspaper or at the court house?
Will we have to have a permit from some official of the State
Board of Health, or of some other body? Should some individual undertake to stop us, what would be our rights?

Cordially yours,

H. T. Hunter, Pres .

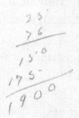

Figure 5. Letter from H. T. Hunter to Dennis G. Brummitt of May 29, 1929, H. T. Hunter
Papers, # HL_MSS16–07_22_366, Special Collections, Hunter Library, Western
Carolina University.

Figure 6. AME Zion Church in 2022. Photo by Liz Harper. Used by permission.

action that took place in the past. Only one student who spoke about the church in the responses did not express negative feelings about the school's choices. Instead, the student felt that the positive outcomes regarding the school's expansion onto the church property did not play a big enough role in the soundwalk script.

On the sounds of the former AME Zion Church site, several participants observed the overall quietude of the current space and linked this to the historic silencing of the church community. As one student put it during the post-walk discussion at the Catafount, "The Zion church is something that no one talks about. Its history is silenced. And we are standing here and even the sounds themselves are leaving a legacy that the elites want us to remember because when we started this walk, we started with the clock bell tolling [at the nearby Alumni Tower]. And there was a bell at that church that no longer rings because it was forcibly torn down." Another participant commented, "[The former church site] was quiet. It kind of sounded desolate. It was like an eerie quietness when you couldn't hear any cars." A student responded,

"Although there weren't cars [at the former Zion church site], even up there there's this drone and construction sound. I would always notice it whenever I lived up there. It's just not going to stop." This play between imagining the sounds of historic soundscapes and listening to one's immediate environment surfaces regularly in the post-walk discussions.

Former Cherokee Mound Site

Some university communities have attempted to reintegrate Native American sounds into their campuses in order to confront histories of silencing and erasure. For example, Native American Studies scholar John-Carlos Perea began to teach powwow singing and drumming at San Francisco State University in 2010. Perea states, "To find a space for powwow music within the university soundscape, it is necessary to address the legacy of terror and embarrassment as articulated through religious, social, and political restrictions that have shaped the reception of powwow music among non-Natives."[33] Likewise, the authors believe that addressing the silencing of those sounds at WCU is essential to understanding the "terror and embarrassment" that Native American students, faculty, and staff have experienced on college campuses. By taking participants to the site of the razed Cherokee mound and the "Wi" sculpture, the Sonic Histories soundwalk underscores the longstanding and complicated relationships WCU has had with the nearby Eastern Band of the Cherokee Indian. Soundwalking can transform a mostly symbolic gesture like *Wi* into active thinking about a time in history when indigenous people inhabited the area that is now filled with the sounds of an institution of higher learning, as demonstrated by student responses to the project.

During the post-walk discussion, several students articulated their experience by relating the historic soundscape of the former mound site to the current site through juxtaposition, such as distinguishing "community" sounds in the historic soundscape from "mechanical" sounds in the current soundscape. Others speculated differences in the organization of social space, with particular attention to age groups, gender roles, activities conducted, and conversation topics. Sounds of the former Cherokee site would have included women talking while weaving baskets, voices in the council house, and young men playing stickball in a nearby field. This sonic environment is in stark contrast to the sounds that now frequent the area: conversations about personal and academic topics, phones ringing, music playing from cars, leaf blowers and lawn mowers, construction, and students in the marching band drumline practicing at the nearby Catafount.

Several students had strong emotional reactions to this site. While students still use words like "uncomfortable" and "sad" to describe the experience, also present are the words "guilt" and "heartbreaking." These students reported feeling the loss of the Cherokee people's home and place deeply. One student even felt a current sense of how racism affects the school and the university's culture by remarking that this history had been "hidden" from the students. And finally, one student—surprised by the history—felt that they will continue to be mindful of this knowledge every time they pass the sculpture, stating, "I was struck by all the history that I encountered. Now, when I walk through campus, I will always remember things like the Native American mound that used to exist where Killian now stands."

Catafount Site

Arguably, the timeline of racialized events at a site impacts students' interactions with that space. This is demonstrated by the Catafount, the site of the most recent racialized events discussed on the soundwalk. Constructed in 2011, the fountain—surrounded by a small brick and concrete amphitheater—became the center for campus social activities such as concerts, Greek life events, flash mobs, vigils, protests, and impromptu gatherings (Figure 7). In 2016, during the height of political tensions on campus revolving around the election that pitted Hillary Clinton against Donald Trump, as well as rising contention surrounding the Black Lives Matter movement (BLM), the WCU campus found itself in what students and faculty referred to as a "chalking war," with students scrawling their beliefs and slogans on the sidewalks near the Catafount. Students discussed the chalking incidents on social media. Some felt their safety was threatened and their sense of belonging to be questioned by chalkings that berated BLM that quoted one of candidate Trump's popular anti-immigrant refrains at his campaign rallies: "Build the Wall," referring to the constructed barrier between the

Figure 7. Campus event at the Catafount. "Division of Student Affairs 2016–2017 Annual Report", 3. *https://www.wcu.edu/WebFiles/FY17-Student-Affairs-Annual-Report.pdf*.

Figure 8. Black Lives Matter student protestors at the Catafount. Photo by WLOS staff. Rex Hodge, "WCU Students Silently Protest Police Shooting in Charlotte" (September 23, 2016), *https://wlos.com/news/local/wcu-students-silently-protest-police-shooting-in-charlotte.*

United States and Mexico. In response to the chalking war, students supporting BLM staged a silent protest at the Catafount (Figure 8). They were approached by students who disagreed with their protest, berated them, and in one case, spat on another student protester.

Fewer students had transformative experiences at the Catafount than at other sites. One student reported talking about the 2016 protests with a friend, one mentioned that they pay more attention to sounds at the site, and one other said—after the soundwalk—that they do not like all the protests occurring there. Most participants simply did not mention that this site was impactful. This lack of interest at this particular site highlights what may be a limitation of our project: familiar sites that have had recent divisive exclusionary events may not transform the students' perceptions of the site's soundscape as substantially as other historic sites, because they have become accustomed to these sounds. However, for the reason that BLM protests and counter-protests are still a regular occurrence in this community and around the United States, it is possible that hearing about the mistreatment of BLM protesters was more likely to elicit pre-existing political positions rather than empathy for those who have been mistreated in the more distant past. This suggests that a combination of sites with different characteristics is necessary for a soundwalk exploring racialized soundscapes. Visiting multiple sites presents a more nuanced picture of how students experience campus history through sound.

CHALLENGING THE TRIUMPHANT NARRATIVE

Sonic Histories demonstrates that students, overall, report that soundwalking is a valuable experience and that listening to the narrative and ambient sounds at these sites allowed them to consider how events at these sites have shaped the university's culture. The authors further posit that soundwalks can challenge institutional perpetuation of the triumphant narrative, and find some evidence in our survey responses that this did occur. This section presents these findings in two parts: first, whether the student recognized the university's past or present racist policy choices, and second whether the student recognized their own complicity in the preservation of these policy choices.

Recognizing the Harmful Effect of University Policies

Students who participated in our soundwalk showed some evidence of recognizing how university policies have contributed to systemic racism on our campus and in our students' and faculties' lives (see Figure 9). They noted underlying racism in some of the choices the authors highlight on the walk, along with disbelief or difficulty coping with the university's choices. One student noted that these negative, racially-driven events had been hidden by university policy. These strong emotions even went so far as being called heartbreaking. The authors posit that this first step, acknowledgment that institutional choices perpetuate discrimination on campus then and now, is an important goal of our soundwalk and that it challenges the triumphant narrative at our university.

Recognizing Individual Complicity

Our second goal, recognizing one's own individual complicity in institutional policies that perpetuate racism, also shows promise in

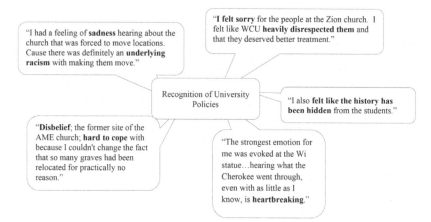

"I had a feeling of **sadness** hearing about the church that was forced to move locations. Cause there was definitely an **underlying racism** with making them move."

"**I felt sorry** for the people at the Zion church. I felt like WCU **heavily disrespected them** and that they deserved better treatment."

Recognition of University Policies

"I also **felt like the history has been hidden** from the students."

"**Disbelief**; the former site of the AME church; **hard to cope** with because I couldn't change the fact that so many graves had been relocated for practically no reason."

"The strongest emotion for me was evoked at the Wi statue…hearing what the Cherokee went through, even with as little as I know, is **heartbreaking**."

Figure 9. Evidence of Student Recognition of University Policies that Contribute to Systemic Racism.

student responses to our survey about the soundwalk (see Figure 10). Students report feeling as if they personally had desecrated sacred land by participating in university activities, strong connections and loss, as well as guilt at the soundwalk sights. One student said that it was "we" rather than WCU that took "things" from people who were harmed in the past. This individual acknowledgment of complicity in harm moves beyond blame toward the university, and shows signs of introspection of how each individual contributes to systemic racism and exclusion.

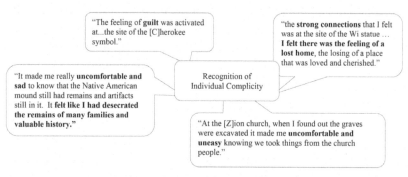

"The feeling of **guilt** was activated at...the site of the [C]herokee symbol."

"the **strong connections** that I felt was at the site of the Wi statue … **I felt there was the feeling of a lost home**, the losing of a place that was loved and cherished."

"It made me really **uncomfortable and sad** to know that the Native American mound still had remains and artifacts still in it. It **felt like I had desecrated the remains of many families and valuable history**."

Recognition of Individual Complicity

"At the [Z]ion church, when I found out the graves were excavated it made me **uncomfortable and uneasy** knowing we took things from the church people."

Figure 10. Evidence of Student Recognition of Individual Complicity that Contribute to Systemic Racism.

CONCLUSIONS

Indeed, gestures such as monuments and plaques give acknowledgement, renewing energy around what is deemed important by those that made the gesture. Still, as long as we are not truly present and listening, silenced voices will remain unheard. As Dylan Robinson observes in his recent book *Hungry Listening*, to listen in a socially conscious way requires a shift from listening *to*, to listening *with*. Robinson advocates for a "resonant theory" of sound studies, whereby "moving away from a conceptualization of the listener as the sole subject in the act of listening, *Hungry Listening* reorients the act toward the life, agency, and subjectivity of sound within Indigenous frameworks of perception."[34] Herein lies a conceptual—if not an ontological—shift from a subject-object interface to a subject-subject one. This resonant theory supports possible future directions in soundwalking and other forms of sound-based research by promoting sonic efficacy. Listening *with* helps establish co-presence and enables empowerment for minority voices. It suggests an awareness of and responsibility to others and at the same time promotes recognition of any self-complicity. Promoting social consciousness through active listening is both necessary and meaningful work, for it calls on one to enter into dialogue with both heard and unheard voices on particularly challenging and painful issues of our times.

Sonic Histories relates the present to the past through critical reflection on the voices of place. This project highlighted the concealed nature of exclusion, prompting discussion of buried stories and silenced voices. Sonic Histories did not prescribe experience, but instead facilitated it. To not listen honestly to the past—whether blindly or by choice—can lead to complacency and therefore enable the perpetuation of racism. Sonic Histories provides a sound-based model that may be used to engage race and racism on the college campus in a respectful, honest, and productive way.

This soundwalk challenged students to listen, engage, and empathize. Although mediated by a portfolio, listening on site to soundscapes that no longer exist was a challenge. As one student remarked after the soundwalk, "I'm still struggling to make the link between history and sound though. Because this is sonic histories, right? . . . what aspect of sonic history is present in the moving of a church or something like that? I'm still kind of trying to get that through my head." A fellow student responded, "I think it really is about connecting, trying to think about how daily life would have been back then, how it would have sounded, and how it could even sound now if history had been different. I mostly was focusing on the sounds I wasn't hearing, sounds I would have heard if I was there. It's a whole different world almost. It feels like a dream." This soundwalk was not a symbolic gesture: it was not passive. This soundwalk was active because it engaged students' emotions, and students reported changed ideas about campus inclusion and diversity, as well as reported these were lasting impressions from the soundwalk. Research shows that this type of active and direct engagement with the soundscape can impact participants' opinions about diversity and equality.[35] As one student put it, "I had strong emotions at every stop. Unpacking the past is always hard, but taking the time and space to be mindful about it in its location was moving in a way that history classes aren't."

The authors found that students both liked the soundwalk and processed empathetic emotions for those harmed by racial discrimination at the selected sites. They had both positive feelings toward *learning* about WCU's history and more negative feelings toward WCU's history. Students appreciated hard truths and processed them in thoughtful ways. Active listening at these sites prompted students to challenge the triumphant narrative, and about half of the participants reported both learning something about systemic racism and a desire to know more. Given our theoretically-driven method and feedback, Sonic Histories demonstrates that soundwalking can be an effective exercise for not only teaching students about diversity and inclusion, but also activating the mindfulness necessary for students to internalize these messages in a positive way.

The authors posit that this impact is both demonstrably substantial and normatively important. The participants expressed a loss of culture from the razed mound and moved church and graves, a feeling of privileged ignorance at not knowing and experiencing the discriminatory history, as well as empathy—and even heartbreak—for the voices who had been silenced and removed before their arrival. A soundwalk, more than a lecture or a general tour, gives students space to not only hear, but to listen and grieve for those voices who could no longer be heard.

In addition to providing evidence that our soundwalk is both well received and triggers active listening by students, the authors further argue that the Sonic Histories soundwalk challenges the triumphant narrative among student participants. Student responses provide evidence that this goal was achieved. Students lamented how histories of and spaces for racial minorities have been removed from WCU, and how these acts—which silence the voices of African Americans and Cherokee, among others—continue to impact today's campus soundscape. Students reported being more aware of the soundscapes of inclusion and exclusion today, and reported instances where they were made aware of exclusion that continues in the present. This soundwalk model can—and arguably should—be used by other institutions to replicate the impact found at WCU, including increased appreciation for and understanding of campus history, interest in histories of racial discrimination, as well as interest in the contemporary impact of racial discrimination on a university campus.

However, it is worth noting that the creation of a soundwalk takes substantial time, planning, and collaboration. This can be accomplished by universities in conjunction with students, faculty, and staff who know that more is needed beyond orientation training and who believe in the effectiveness of data-driven programs designed to address the systemic racism that plagues universities today. A soundwalk project like this requires heavy lifting (historical digging, logistics, and institutional support), but the potential outcomes are well worth the undertaking for those committed to change.

TYLER KINNEAR is an independent researcher in Cambridge, MA. His research interests include sonic art and the environment, histories and theories of listening, and global music studies. His work has been published in *Chigiana: Journal of Musicological Studies, Ecomusicology Review, Intersections: Canadian Journal of Music,* and *Organised Sound.*

ROBERT HUNT FERGUSON is an Associate Professor of History at Western Carolina University where he teaches courses on popular culture, the Cold War, and the American West. His book, *Race and the Remaking of the Rural South: Interracialism, Christian Socialism, and Cooperative Farming in Jim Crow Mississippi* was published with the University of

Georgia Press in 2018. His work has appeared in the *Journal of Southern History*, the *North Carolina Historical Review,* and *Arkansas Historical Quarterly.* His research has been funded by the Center for the Study of the American South and the North Caroliniana Society.

JESSICA M. HAYDEN is an Assistant Professor of Political Science and Public Affairs at Western Carolina University. Her teaching and research interests focus on American political institutions, representation, political communication, and diversity and politics. Her book *Congressional Communication in a Digital Age* was published by Routledge in 2017. Her research has been published in *Social Science Quarterly, Journal of Political Marketing,* and *Albany Government Law Review.*

NOTES

1. This research was made possible by a Western Carolina University Provost's Internal Funding Support Grant and a WCU Faculty Research and Creative Activities Award. We would like to thank the Director of the Office of Student Transitions at WCU, Glenda Hensley, for supporting the "soundwalk" lesson plan (and other diversity modules) by codifying it in University Experience instructor training.
2. Although a soundwalk implies ability in terms of ambulation, audition, and vision, impaired individuals are able to participate if the route is disability friendly. A disability-friendly soundwalk presents a route—and any required assistance—that enables any impaired individual to participate in the exercise safely (e.g., wheelchair access is in place and crosswalks are enabled with accessible pedestrian signals).
3. John Levack Drever, "Soundwalking: Aural Excursions into the Everyday," in *The Ashgate Research Companion to Experimental Music,* ed. James Saunders (Farnham, UK: Ashgate, 2009), 165.
4. Image of printed Yik Yak posts, unprocessed collection, Special Collections, Hunter Library, Western Carolina University.
5. Tyler Kinnear, "Reflections from the Vancouver Soundwalk Collective," *The World Forum for Acoustic Ecology Newsletter* 9, no. 4 (2012): 11; Hildegard Westerkamp, "Soundwalking," *Sound Heritage* 3, no. 4 (1974): 18–27.
6. It is common for organizers to present audio or video recordings or live performance during a soundwalk. For research purposes, we sought to present each site as being storied through the archival materials and therefore did not supplement the soundwalk beyond the use of a portfolio. Enhancing sites with media is something several instructors have applied in course-based soundwalks at WCU. For example, one instructor reported playing era-appropriate African American gospel songs to further stoke students' historical imaginations and understandings of historical erasure. Another instructor mentioned playing excerpts from Adrien Litzau's 2004 interview with sisters Hazel Whiteside and Louise Allen, both members of the AME Zion Church, in which they discuss growing up in the area and attending

the church in the early and mid twentieth century. "Interview with Hazel Whiteside and Louise Allen, 22 October 2004," *WCU Special Collections*, Inventory #: HL_MSS01–04_Litzau_Whiteside_Allen_2004-10-22:4, https://southernappalachian digitalcollections.org/object/36325.

7. Jennifer Lynn Stoever, *The Sonic Color Line: Race and the Cultural Politics of Listening* (New York: New York University Press, 2016), 27.

8. On this topic, see Sarah Justina Eyerly, *Moravian Soundscapes: A Sonic History of the Moravian Missions in Early Pennsylvania* (Bloomington: Indiana University Press, 2020); Konca Saher and Murat Cetin, "Music and Performance as Sonic Acts of Political Struggle; Counter-Political Soundscapes in Urban Realm," *Sociology Study* 6, no. 6 (2016): 378–391; and Alexander Fisher, *Music, Piety, and Propaganda: The Soundscapes of Counter-Reformation Bavaria* (Oxford: Oxford University Press, 2014).

9. For more on the history of the WSP and current directions in the field of acoustic ecology, see Milena Droumeva and Randolph Jordan, eds., *Sound, Media, Ecology* (Cham: Palgrave Macmillan, 2019).

10. On applications of soundwalking in cultural ethnography, see Ozgun Eylul İşcen, "In-Between Soundscapes of Vancouver: The Newcomer's Acoustic Experience of a City with a Sensory Repertoire of Another Place," *Organised Sound* 19, no. 2 (2014): 125–135; Jennifer Schine, "Listening to a Sense of Place: Acoustic Ethnography with Billy Proctor in the Broughton Archipelago, British Columbia" (Master's thesis, Simon Fraser University, 2013); Helmi Järviluoma, "Lesconil, My Home: Memories of Listening," in *Acoustic Environments in Change*, ed. H. Järviluoma, M. Kytö, B. Truax, H. Uimonen, and N. Vikman (Tampere, Finland: TAMK University of Applied Sciences, 2009): 172–192; in education, see Amanda M. Black and Andrea F. Bohlman, "Resounding the Campus: Pedagogy, Race, and the Environment," *Journal of Music History Pedagogy* 8, no. 1 (2017): 6–27; Adam Tinkle, "Sound Pedagogy: Teaching Listening Since Cage," *Organized Sound* 20, no. 2 (2015): 220–230; and Andra McCartney, "Performing Soundwalks for Journées Sonores, Canal de Lachine," in *Performing Nature: Explorations in Ecology and the Arts*, eds. Gabriella Giannachi and Nigel Stewart (Bern: Peter Lang, 2005): 217–234; in geography, see Toby Butler, "A Walk of Art: The Potential of the Sound Walk as Practice in Cultural Geography," *Social & Cultural Geography* 7, no. 6 (2006): 889–908; in sonic art, see Georgios Varoutsos, "Peace Wall Belfast: Spatial Audio Representation of Divided Spaces and Soundwalks," (Proceedings of the 17th Sound and Music Computing Conference, Torino, Italy, June 24–26, 2020): 123–130; Yolande Harris, "Presentness in Displaced Sound," *Leonardo Music Journal* 23 (2013): 13–14; and Christoph Cox and Christina Kubisch, "Invisible Cities: An Interview with Christina Kubisch," *Cabinet Magazine* 21 (2006): http://cabinetmagazine.org/issues/21/cox.php and in urban planning, see Mags Adams, "Hearing the City: Reflections on Soundwalking," *Qualitative Researcher* 10 (2009): 6–9; and W.J. Davies, R. Cain, A. Carlyle, D.A. Hall, K.I. Hume, and C.J. Plack, "The positive soundscape project: A synthesis of results from many disciplines," in *Internoise Innovations in Practical Noise Control* (Ottawa, Canada, August 23–26, 2009): 1–8.

11. On voyeurism and art-based performance, see David Shearing, "Intimacy, Immersion and the Desire to Touch: The Voyeur Within," in *Theatre as Voyeur-*

ism, ed. George Rodosthenous (London: Palgrave Macmillan, 2015): 71–87, doi: 10.1057/9781137478818_4.

12. Mitchell Akiyama, "Unsettling the World Soundscape Project: Soundscapes of Canada and the Politics of Self-Recognition," *Sounding Out!* (blog, August 20, 2015): https://soundstudiesblog.com/2015/08/20/unsettling-the-world-soundscape-project-soundscapes-of-canada-and-the-politics-of-self-recognition/.

13. Allie Martin, "Hearing Change in the Chocolate City: Soundwalking as Black Feminist Method," *Sounding Out!* (blog, August 5, 2019): https://soundstudiesblog.com/2019/08/05/hearing-change-in-the-chocolate-city-soundwalking-as-black-feminist-method/; Leah Sandals, "Step by Step: Artists Walk to Resist Colonization, Ableism and More," *Canadian Art* (June 22, 2017): https://canadianart.ca/features/step-step-artists-walk-resist-colonization-ableism/.

14. Dylan Robinson, *Hungry Listening: Resonant Theory for Indigenous Sound Studies* (Minneapolis: University of Minnesota Press, 2020); John-Carlos Perea, "Native 'Noise' and the Politics of Powwow Musicking in a University Soundscape," in *Music and Modernity Among First Peoples of North America*, eds. Victoria Lindsay Levine and Dylan Robinson (Middletown, CT: Wesleyan University Press, 2019): 142–157; Dustin Tahmahkera, "Becoming Sound: Tubitsinakukuru from Mt. Scott to Standing Rock," *Sounding Out!* (blog, October 9, 2017): https://soundstudiesblog.com/2017/10/09/becoming-sound-tubitsinakukuru-from-mt-scott-to-standing-rock/ Nimalan Yoganathan, "Disparate Soundscapes and Ecotones: Critically Sounding the Amazon and Arctic" (Master's thesis, Concordia University 2017); and John Wynne, "Hearing Voices: Research and creative practice across cultures and disciplines," *Language Documentation and Description* 12 (2014): 120–150.

15. Black and Bohlman, "Resounding the Campus"; and Varoutsos, "Peace Wall Belfast." This application of soundwalking is part of a growing interest in sound-based methods of inquiry into racialized spaces. Examples in the southeastern US include entries in the *Southern Cultures* special issue, "The Sonic South" (Winter 2021), and Kevin Kehrberg and Jeffrey A. Keith's multimedia project on music, history, race, and labor in Western North Carolina, available at https://bittersoutherner.com/2020/somebody-died-babe-a-musical-coverup-of-racism-violence-and-greed.

16. Both Black and Bohlman's and Varoutsos's projects are fundamentally artistic in their approach. Graduate students in Bohlman's musicology seminar created nine scores informed by historical documents from the UNC University Archives, which were then performed at specific sites during a soundwalk, titled Beyond the Belltower, by undergraduate students in Bohlman's Music and Politics class. Varoutsos directs participants in his Peace Wall Belfast Soundwalks to listen to binaural recordings of real-world sounds around the Peace Wall Belfast over headphones while tracing the predetermined route of his walk.

17. Heather Menefee, "Black Activist Geographies: Teaching Whiteness as Territoriality on Campus," *South: A Scholarly Journal* 50, no. 2 (2018): 167–186.

18. The Cherokee are one of the indigenous people of what is now the southeastern United States. Most Cherokee were forcibly relocated in the 1830s to the southwestern US by the federal government. In the 1870s, Cherokee who had evaded removal purchased land in their homeland, known as the Qualla Boundary.

19. Robert Lee and Tristan Ahtone, "Land-grab Universities: Expropriated Indigenous Land is the Foundation of the Land Grant University," *High Country News* (March 30, 2020): https://www.hcn.org/issues/52.4/indigenous-affairs-education-land-grab-universities.

20. Lucas P. Kelley and Garrett W. Wright, "Without profit from stolen Indigenous lands, UNC would have gone broke 100 years ago," *Scalawag* (September 15, 2020): https://scalawagmagazine.org/2020/09/indian-land-university-profit.

21. WCU's history is inextricably bound up in the illegal seizure of Cherokee land and the social Darwinist ideas of the Jim Crow era. The land that now houses WCU was a hub of the Cherokee community until 1819, when North Carolina forcefully pushed a treaty that ceded the land to the state. From the 1820s to the 1860s, the land was worked by African American enslaves laborers until emancipation. In the 1880s, the Cullowhee Academy, as it was known then, was founded on the eve of the Jim Crow era.

22. Lillian Hirst, "Old Indian Mound Being Levelled At WCC Yielding Relics Of Past," *Asheville Citizen-Times* (NC) (June 24, 1956): 8B.

23. Jacquelyn Dowd Hall, "The Long Civil Rights Movement and the Political Uses of the Past," *Journal of American History* 91, no. 4 (2005): 1234.

24. Hall, "The Long Civil Rights Movement and the Political Uses of the Past," 1235.

25. See, "Diversity Through the Years," WCU Heritage and History, https://www.wcu.edu/engage/mountain-heritage-center/heritage-and-history/diversity.aspx This narrative of inclusive excellence continues to be promoted in university publications. See, for example, Bill Studenc, "Winds of Change," *Western Carolina University Magazine* (Fall 2020): 26–39, available at https://www.wcu.edu/stories/posts/winds-of-change.aspx.

26. Jerry Bembry, "How Hoops Legend Henry Logan Overcame Injuries, Alcholism, and Illitarcy," *Andscape* (5 September 2018); Garrett Moore, "Garrett Moore, BSUL President Interviewed For EXPRESSION," The Black Expression (Spring Quarter 1971): 3. While the student body became slightly more diverse in the 1960s, by the 1970s, the African American population on campus was still low compared to other regional comprehensive universities. In 1970, African American students made up roughly one percent of the student body. Yet, this small contingent of students actively and effectively advocated for more representation on campus. In the spring of 1970, Black Students United for Liberation (now the Black Student Union) submitted a list of demands to the WCU administration. The demands included "admission of more black students, hiring of more black instructors, black administrative staff members, a black studies program, black speakers and lectures, and the removal of race from room assignment applications." By the fall of 1970, three departments—English, History, and Political Science—had established classes in African American literature, history, and civil rights. Yet, black representation on campus remained low. By 1973, black students had risen to only two and a half percent of the total student body.

27. Dagan LaMont Burrell, "All Quiet at the Western Front: a History of Black/White Relations at Western Carolina University" (Master's thesis, Western Carolina University, 1992): 39–40.

28. Burrell, "All Quiet at the Western Front," 40.

29. Mark M. Smith, "Echo," in *Keywords in Sound*, eds. David Novak and Matt Sakakenny (Durham: Duke University Press, 2015): 55–64.
30. "2020 Student Body Profile," https://www.wcu.edu/_images/learn/provost /WCU_2020_Student_Body_Profile.pdf.
31. Gabriel R. Sanchez and Edward D. Vargas, "Taking a Closer Look at Group Identity: The Link between Theory and Measurement of Group Consciousness and Linked Fate," *Political Research Quarterly* 69, no. 1 (2016): doi: 10.1177/1065912915624571.
32. Rakhi Ruparelia, "Guilty Displeasures: White Resistance in the Social Justice Classroom," *Dalhousie Law Journal* 37, no. 2 (2014): 815–845.
33. Perea, "Native 'Noise' and the Politics of Powwow Musicking in a University Soundscape," 155.
34. Robinson, *Hungry Listening*, 15.
35. Vincent Andrisani, "'¡Se Bota El Tanque!': housing, infrastructure, and the sounds of water in Havana's domestic spaces," *Tapuya: Latin American Science, Technology and Society* 2, no. 1 (2019): 442–457; and Tripta Chandola, "Listening in to water routes: Soundscapes as cultural systems," *International Journal of Cultural Studies* 16, no. 1 (2012): 55–69.

Reinhabiting Ecotopia

Weaving the Threads of People, Place, and Possibilities

RANDALL AMSTER

Abstract

In the face of escalating environmental and social crises, this essay explores how it might be possible to reweave the threads that connect people to one another, collectively to place, and jointly toward possible futures. Highlighting the potential of a renewed human-environment interface across a range of perspectives and illustrations, and drawing upon concepts such as reinhabitation and practices of placemaking, it is considered here how making connections with people and places that might otherwise be taken for granted can help foster more grounded experiences and cultivate imaginations at the same time. Confronting apparent assertions from some quarters that humankind must move further away from "nature" to address current crises, the central aim of this intervention is to examine how a commitment toward deeper engagement with the world around us can stoke aspirations and attitudes for positive change.

> We can only choose between worlds
> We have already variously altered and harmed
> And we do not lack the gas to get away
> But lack the imagination of another
> Way of inhabiting space
>
> —Stephen Collis, Once in *Blockadia*[1]

REINTRODUCTION

A recent article in *Forbes Magazine* matter-of-factly reported that "nature can no longer sustain us" and that food systems will have to be "decoupled from nature" to meet current and future needs.[2] It is difficult to imagine a more pointed (if unintended) commentary on how far modern societies have drifted from the texture of living systems, as the 'solution' proposed to the problem of profound disconnection is to fully disconnect. Ideas like this carry the imprimatur of progress and innovation, emphasizing high-tech interpolations in a world already ravaged by mechanistic thinking and technocratic incursions. At the same time, there is a concomitant renaissance of back-to-the-land movements and exemplars that point in another direction, one that is neither anti-progress nor retrogressive in its approach. It is, rather, time-tested and rooted in ecology.

This essay will not comprise a litany of these emerging and inspiring examples, nor will it attempt to synthesize best practices from these movements and networks (subjects that are well-documented in manifold texts and case studies in the field). Instead, the aim here is to uncover and explicate the 'software' that underscores the myriad of community-based, egalitarian, decolonizing, closed-loop, decentralized, participatory, and sustainable projects underway in urban and rural contexts from the local to the global scales. Look for these initiatives, support them, join them, start one, and make those connections durable and diverting wherever you can. And in so doing, consider the larger frame of many societies being "decoupled from nature" and its implications—and how it might be possible to reweave the threads that connect people to one another, collectively to place, and jointly toward possible futures.

The purpose of this intervention is to highlight the potential of a vigorous human-environment interface that seeks to (1) illuminate the boundary in order to recognize it before it becomes permanently severed and (2) problematize the boundary in order to reclaim humanity's place within the web while there is still time to do so. Drawing upon concepts such as *reinhabitation* and practices of *placemaking*, combined with *ecotopian* aspirations, the aim is to address deeply rooted structural issues that undergird the mounting, intersecting crises of this era. In this work, it is often the case that the hardest changes to make are the ones closest to home, but they also tend to yield the greatest benefits when successful. A spirit of deeply rooted interconnections and ongoing vigilance is essential for reminding us in no uncertain terms that a better world is possible, that it is already emerging in real time, that any vision of utopia is always under construction, and that the future is defined not by remote bureaucrats but by those who boldly carve a path simply by traversing it. With this spirit of grounded imagination in hand, it becomes plausible to embark on the task of deep reconnection.

EASY BEING GREEN?

One may look upon scenes of pristine nature with awe, reverence, longing, perhaps even love. Iconic topographies beckon, kindling naturalistic feelings of ecological belonging, stoking the fires of conservationism, and inviting us into their verdant embrace. Whether the Grand Canyon or a local trail, a stoic backyard tree or a walk in the park on a sunny day, nature has a way of reaching our inner core unlike any other stimuli encountered. This can sometimes manifest in celebratory reflections, ecstatic ruminations, poetic invocations, and other forms of intense affiliation with *place*. Indeed, "place profoundly shapes our emotional lives" as to everyday events and dramatic episodes alike, providing a potential mechanism for connecting individual experiences to societal change.[3] Such visceral moments can spark alterations in ourselves and our world, in the recognition that being "more transported" in this manner can bring "greater attitude and belief changes," as Alexa Weik von Mossner pertinently discerns in *Affective Ecologies*.[4]

When one thinks of 'nature writing' it is often conceived unidirectionally: *people writing about nature*. But nature inscribes itself upon us as well, writing itself into our psyches, bringing to light the wilderness within and rekindling the call of the wild buried under centuries of domestication. This isn't your grandparents' nostalgic *nature* anymore, separate and apart from human doings and typifying what von Mossner terms "a false dichotomy between nature and culture."[5] This feeling instead is a vibrant reminder of an inherent interconnection with all things, all beings, every molecule, every person, all times, all places. It is the indelible glow of a day at the beach, a hike up the peak, a retreat to the woods, a glimpse of the wild, and everyday sustenance alike. If the experience of modern life often is one of disposability, nature immersions can center indispensability instead.

This all plays well enough as either poetry or prose, laden with moving verbiage and imagery. Experiences of pristine nature are an invitation to reflect and grow, to reconnect and emote, to find solace in a world seemingly gone mad with crises and consumption. Yet there is also a keen awareness of the implications, historical and contemporary, the "violent dispossession" and "the troubling link between nature conservation and colonial attempts to control populations," as Irma Allen pointedly notes in an essay on "The Trouble with Rewilding . . ."[6] What of the spaces already disturbed, the ones trodden and besotted, mined and malled, exploited and despoiled? We might honor vibrant leaders and verdant landscapes, but what of the imperfect and impacted? Climbing a mountain yields inspiration; traversing a food desert brings desperation. "Embodied cognition," as von Mossner implies,[7] may be most welcome when things are well-packaged.

Green environmentalism sometimes infers a sense of splendor that stokes feelings of affiliation and urges a longing for Edenic experiences. Closer in, however, imperfections emerge, scars are revealed, and the sober reckoning of complicity by many of us with destructiveness is rendered apparent. These are the parts just outside the camera's gaze, the ones not posted on social media feeds, the scenes left on the cutting-room floor by the ruthless editors of comportment and profitability. "What emerges in damaged landscapes . . . ?" inquires Anna Lowenhaupt Tsing in *The Mushroom at the End of the World,* when we confront a reality of "living despite economic and ecological ruination"—yet somehow, perhaps, finding in this an impetus toward "collaborative survival."[8]

Anticipating these looming challenges, Ernest Callenbach, the erstwhile author of the genre-founding 1970s novels *Ecotopia* and *Ecotopia Emerging,* wrote in a final missive before his passing in April 2012: "There is beauty in weathered and unpainted wood, in orchards overgrown, even in abandoned cars being incorporated into the earth. Let us learn, like the Forest Service sometimes does, to put unwise or unneeded roads 'to bed,' help a little in the healing of the natural contours, the re-vegetation by native plants. Let us embrace decay, for it is the source of all new life and growth."[9] In this spirit the essential duality of our existence is broached, caught within a dialectic of growth and decay, of creation and destruction, of life and death. Places hold these polarities in a dynamic yet stable tension, across swaths of time.

In the influential volume *Braiding Sweetgrass,* Robin Wall Kimmerer reminds us that "even a wounded world holds us."[10] That embrace is more than a metaphor; it literally is the case in terms of gravity and atmosphere and oceanic tides and land on which to flourish. Everything we are, have known, and will be has its origins in the earth, as a part of the larger cosmos—our part. The planet is a myriad of unique interdependent ecosystems, and also is a unitary biome unto itself. When we scale out to the global view, even glimpsing our world from the tenuous vantage point of near space, we can recognize the power and fragility of our blue-green marble. The astronauts who witness this might have gone forth as pilots but they sometimes return as poets. It is an emotional experience to recognize this deep sense of belonging, of being home.

REKINDLING INHABITATION

This is the essence of *reinhabitation,* the capacity to fall back in love with *place* and, in the process, with humankind as well. To do so, there really cannot be any (or at least, not *many*) exceptions: it is problematic to proclaim our love for the pristine and polished while rejecting the damaged and disturbed. Reinhabitation is about reconnecting with the whole of creation by embracing unconditionally our particular part of its total tapestry, not simply cherry-picking a halcyon place where cherries still blossom on warm spring days. This means affirming allegiance not merely for the penitent but also for those within the penitentiary, not just for things that are green but also for those touched by greed. We don't get to decide which parts are more valuable or worthy than others—in an interlinked world, all of the constituent pieces, people, and places matter on some level.

This sort of expansive thinking challenges our conceptions of right and wrong, good and evil, beauty and horror. It may well be within our nature to seek 'the good' as societies have come to define it, yet surely that judgment is rife with cultural imprints that many of us are scarcely aware of on a conscious level—constituting a form of implicit bias that would be objectionable if coded under more invidious terms. Applying this sensibility to place, Joshua Lockyer and James R. Veteto posited in the introduction to their volume on *Environmental Anthropology Engaging Ecotopia:* "Reinhabitation entails a process whereby individuals and communities decide to commit themselves to a particular bioregion and live 'as if' their descendants will be living there thousands of years into the future. The antithesis of the current global economic system, which rewards hypermobility and jumping at the chance for quick profit, reinhabitation means doing what is best for the long-term health and viability of the socioecological community."[11]

Such calls are critical for expanding conceptions of both space and time as spheres in which actions have repercussions beyond immediate impacts. In this sense, we find that the particular and the universal are always already connected. One can study the macroscopic features of a place, reporting on suburbanization or commercialization trends for instance, discerning large-scale patterns of human communication and conveyance—or we can view things microcosmically from the perspective of one cobblestone seamlessly taking in history from below. We can survey the heavens in search of alien life and other worlds—or just zoom in on the miraculous journey of a single grain of sand. We can long for and illuminate the workings of utopian experiments—or just reach out in solidarity to a single person. We can make a pilgrimage to a specifically 'sacred' place—or just find it everywhere.

Words matter in this regard, helping to open vistas in our minds to match the ones in nature. Writing and speaking in the burgeoning days of modern environmental mobilizations (c. 1970), influential Beat poet and Buddhist ecologist Gary Snyder propagated the idea of reinhabitation to encapsulate a sense of grounded awe that could help (re)connect people to place—and to *all* places. The term is intended to convey a spirit of reconnection to our histories and societies through *placemaking,* cultivating "specific ways to *be*" that are relevant and appropriate to local ecosystems, as Snyder suggests.[12] However, this does not imply a dose of parochialism or stagnation; as John Charles Ryan has noted, "this is not utopian provincialism hiding within watershed boundaries,"[13] but rather is a form of ingenuity. In this light, reinhabitation is about being locally rooted *and* globally resonant, cultivating horizontal networks across topographies.

The concept of reinhabitation also has helped to shape critiques of colonization through the use of placed-based pedagogies in spaces of displacement and dislocation, as Alexa Scully explored in an article for the *Canadian Journal of Environmental Education.* This isn't an attempt to revise history or carry its baggage in a virtuous manner but rather, as Scully opined, "it is an effort to resist the continuing oppression of the colonizing structures of global capitalist economy, and to generate healthier people and land in a way that honors and respects interrelationship."[14] Such constructions are conceptually connected to notions of bioregionalism (as suggested above) by placing an emphasis on viewing cultures and peoples through their deep relations to place and time—including re-reading "sacred stories" from multiple traditions through an ecological lens, as Matthew Humphrey opined in an article on "Reinhabiting Place."[15]

Illustrating these points is the *acequia* water-sharing system in the arid southwestern United States (which bears similarities to collaborative irrigation models found around the world). The acequias generally are earthen irrigation ditches that carry snowmelt into the desert valleys, providing this essential life-giving infusion to farms and communities. Beyond these tangible resource allocations is a deeply rooted ethos of shared labor, participatory governance, collective placemaking, and a strong sense of mutual interdependence among the water users and with the land itself. This system has been in place for centuries, but increasingly is under pressure from development and commercial interests in the region who covet the water as a commodity. Despite these pressures, as Devon Peña has observed, the acequia remains "the material and spiritual embodiment of people making habitable places" and represents a "profound recollection and rearticulation of a sense of place by local cultures."[16]

In her book *Acequia,* Sylvia Rodríguez considers placemaking as "both narrative and practice," viewing the production of a sense of locality as "a structure of feeling" that inscribes itself on individuals and communities through practices including resource sharing and governance.[17] In this sense, the "practices of place" come to produce "local subjects" who embody the patterns of their communities as they are situated in material activities.[18] The acequia is an intriguing and even quintessential exemplar of how a more direct nexus between people and place in practical and ideal terms can provide a template for reconnecting societies at scale to the world around us in all of its manifestations. As Peña concludes, the acequias "are restoring their own place-based identities while struggling to reinhabit disturbed places," epitomizing the environmental justice objective of "reinhabitation of violated places."[19]

Extending these insights, a central tenet of reinhabitation emerges in the insistence of cultivating "long-term reciprocal engagement" between the human and nonhuman elements of place, as Lawrence Buell observed in *Writing for an Endangered World*.[20] A robust sense of reciprocity is more than just recognizing that things are interconnected; it entails compassion and empathy as well. These "thick" forms of affective engagement, von Mossner notes,[21] elicit a tendency toward responsibility rather than reaction, and a concomitant spirit of solidarity rather than sympathy. These more advanced forms of grounded emotive engagement can help build actionable impulses from wistful longings, turning appreciation into activism and worldviews into world-building efforts. As Tsing concludes, paying attention in deep ways to the world around us might not be enough by itself to stave off impending crises—"but it might open our imaginations."[22]

ADVANCED PLACEMENTS

This work is aided by "the rich attachments and affective bonds we have to the environment," as Kimberly Skye Richards writes in an essay on *solastalgia* (i.e., distress caused by myriad negative impacts on the environment) in the volume *An Ecotopian Lexicon*—but it doesn't happen in a vacuum.[23] Richards observes that such bonding can emerge in a "dystopian world [as] a response to the endangerment, extinction, habitat loss, enclosure, and privatization" that is being registered everywhere but is experienced acutely in places heavily impacted by colonialist processes.[24] Still, despite this, Richards urges that it is critical to remember that "not all is lost" and that "places must not be abandoned because they are not perfect;" in this manner, harm can yield healing by focusing on "developing a loving relationship with a place."[25]

Extending the logic of placemaking and embodied affinity, the notion of *ecotopia* appears as a correlate of reinhabitation—even as it is sometimes (mis)taken for its final destination, which is actually is an "ahistorical and abstract" rendering of the utopian impulse.[26] Ecotopia is more so about experimentation, nurturing an open-endedness that flies in the face of inevitability and futility, and a radical reclaiming of hope expressed through "the readiness to go to any length to restore community," as suggested by the iconic Grace Lee Boggs.[27] The impulse to restore ourselves and the world—not to some pristine past, but rather to be informed by what has been in order to reclaim the capacity to fashion a future together—is an ongoing endeavor. Connecting to places mutualistically can help to heal ourselves through the work of restoration.

In fact, it may be that passion for "a vulnerable ecological space that is at risk," as von Mossner deduces,[28] is a requisite antidote to the far more pernicious mindset of complacency in the face of calamity. To the extent that ecotopia conveys an active process and a vision that is neither static nor finalized, it can provide a motivating future-oriented aspiration rather than a regressive nostalgia to make something 'great' in our minds while denying the stark realities of past and present practices. In this way, we can reinhabit time as well as space. Indeed, places have layers, stratigraphically and temporally, where the inscribed natural and cultural histories of the people who have lived there ahead of displacing forces can be read, those whose labor built the soils and the wealth of nations, and the tribulations of present inhabitants as they cope with forces including gentrification, toxification, homogenization, and much more.

Despite how perilous the future seems, the aim is not to pursue a reinhabited ecotopia that takes us backward, but rather one that stokes dreams and visions going forward. To keep this from becoming an exercise in academic abstraction, or merely a conversation that leads nowhere, there is a need for momentum and action, the impetus and wherewithal to make change, a reinvigoration of a keen sense of place and a commitment to cultivate it wherever we find ourselves. Sometimes this effort might manifest as a "pocket utopia" that, in its best sense, represents an ephemeral experience in which "we make and are made by" the web of relationships that comprise the world, as Vandana Singh observes in *Utopias of the Third Kind*.[29] Despite their fleeting nature, pocket utopias can help cultivate resistance to what Singh terms the "reality trap" of truncated imagination.[30] Experiments in different ways of being and living, including experiences of stepping outside the constructed norms of business as usual—from urban community gardens to backcountry trail excursions, and more—can be grounding and help form new pathways.

The careful balancing of integration and impermanence is critical for any attempt at vibrant placemaking. Rather than viewing these poles as dichotomous, it can be surmised that eternal change is enabled rather than constrained by the combination of stability and continuity—and that the opposite is also true, namely that a durable and sustainable community is one with a penchant for diversification and adaptiveness. Experiences of ephemeral pocket utopias can serve multiple purposes, from liberating imaginations and giving us glimpses of another path, to making new connections with people and places that might otherwise be taken for granted. In this spirit, the collected volume *All We Can Save* includes an essay by Christine E. Nieves Rodriguez succinctly fixing on what is needed to weather the storms now at hand, and those rapidly emerging: "The times we will be facing are going to require us to recognize that the most important thing around us is community."[31]

ROCKS AND ROCKETS

Leaning into a strong sense of community immediately asks us to expand the notion to include more-than-human components. Some classical environmentalists, like Aldo Leopold, recognized the necessity for humankind to reinvigorate its embeddedness within the community of life, to reframe our relative positionality from that of dominance to interdependence, to recognize our inherent intertwining with one another and the world of which we are a part.[32] None of this is groundbreaking unto itself—but rather, it is *ground-making*. Land, as Leopold urges, represents "a fountain of energy" uniting soil, plants, and animals.[33] And building fertile soils is more than simply composting; it also entails imbuing awareness of living systems and dynamic exchange into the process. Interacting sustainably and equitably with our communities and world isn't merely a matter of better distribution of material benefits and burdens; it is likewise a call to embrace the ethos of communion as a function of an inherent reciprocity that binds all things.

A concrete illustration of this (literally) thus comes by way of what Jane Zelikova asserts is "a precious, disappearing, and resoundingly underappreciated resource: soil."[34] The manifestation of a thin layer of earth as a life-giving strata makes tangible the requisite values of reconnection and restoration: to deplete the soil is to strip bare the capacity of this world to support life. Conversely, when people engage with soil reciprocally and intentionally, they can help be the agents of reinvigorated places. As Zelikova critically observes, however, "there is no technical innovation that can bring soil back,"[35] indicating that only time and biology can keep this critical shell alive. Leah Penniman further notes that "the exploitation of the soil" is a substantial driver of climate change and conditions of human degradation alike, yet also reminds us that the work of building healthy soils can yield therapeutic benefits (physically and emotionally) as well.[36]

Digging deeper, literally and figuratively, calls forth a range of critical insights about the centrality of place and the importance of staying grounded in a time of rampant change. Through the lens of Environmental Justice, it becomes apparent that merely seeking a more equitable distribution within an inherently unsustainable and unjust system is not in itself sufficient. In a climate displacement context, for instance, offering generic acreage to replace what people have lost is a mechanical answer to a complex problem. As Damayanti Banergee writes, places exist beyond mere economic frames as resources and opportunities, and include critical dimensions of politics, power, culture, heritage, narratives, ethics, and experiences that underscore peoples' relationships to one another and with the earth that centers their lives.[37] Aspects of individual affect and social interactions provide a grounding for navigating uncertain times and the challenges of a world that sometimes seems as if it is slipping away in real time.

Against the necessity of soil rehabilitation and grounding in place, it is worth considering how a space colonization fantasy can serve as a cosmic escape hatch for transcending a perilous and precarious world, deigning to relieve us of the clear and present obligation to restore what we have wreaked on this planet (albeit not all of us equally, as the benefits and burdens of myriad behaviors have been skewed along a range of geographical and demographic factors). The basic messaging of the do-over mindset sometimes in evidence with space colonization really isn't all that subtle, as it plays out in a wide range of science fiction treatments and tangible aspirations: *it's too late for this old world, and our destiny is in the heavens anyway.* Extrapolating the implicit logic at hand: *Space gives us a do-over, a second chance, a clean slate; those who*

came before us and started down this path didn't have the tools to build
ladders to the sky, but we do and we're clever and resourceful enough to
get it right somewhere out there—rather than futilely trying to rehabil-
itate a rapidly decaying world.

Science ostensibly affirms the underlying premise, in the sense of conveying the scope and urgency of the challenge at hand, pointing to 'planetary boundaries' as to basic ecosystem services and core bio-processes that have been (or are in imminent danger of being) crossed, perhaps irreversibly, and the implications of moving into a world that might scarcely resemble the one in which modern societies have developed.[38] The earth indeed is in crisis, at least in terms of its capacity to continue supporting humans and complex life in general, and the challenge of what it might be like to start over out there may seem preferable to the hard work of cleaning up the mess on the home front. Out there is what it could have been like if we had gotten it together here— but alas, humankind was predestined to foul its nest, or so goes the dominant narrative that reinforces the notion that "humans and nature were a bad mix."[39] Indeed, it often appears that the spate of looming crises, of which we have barely skimmed the surface of full impacts, threaten to impinge not only the habitat but the ability to navigate a way forward with dignity and compassion. Hence it might be said, in the space-faring vernacular: *humans, we have a problem.*

JUST TECHNOLOGY?

The "rocks versus rockets" motif, with its contrasting aspects of being grounded or taking flight, raises an equally fundamental question about the role of technology in the reclamation of place and space. It is often said that technology is value-free, in the sense that it is neither good nor bad on its own terms, and that any ethical implications are dependent upon what we do with it. The frontiers of scientific advancement mainly are pushed within arenas set apart from cultural discourse or metaphysical reflection, leaving issues in those realms to be processed outside of the laboratories and research sites. Once a technology advances beyond the lab and enters the market, scientists can do little more to influence the course of its ethical impacts than an artist can control how people interpret their work. One may even win a Nobel Prize for their efforts, yet have limited sway over the range of applications to which their work is plied in the world. Many scientists, of course, are guided by ethical frameworks that encourage working for the betterment of humankind, and indeed some of the figures noted here (including Rachel Carson) staked their careers on using their platform for good, rendering these issues in a complex way.

The challenge is how the technologies developed from scientific inquiries often find their way into a wide range of uses (and users) without sufficient societal discourse. Considering these ramifications, Martin Luther King Jr. expressed a perspective that still stands as a forceful forewarning about the potential for our fascination with technology to eclipse our sense of morality: "We have to face the fact that modern man suffers from a kind of poverty of the spirit, which stands in glaring contrast to his scientific and technological abundance. We've learned to fly the air like birds, we've learned to swim the seas like fish, and yet we haven't learned to walk the Earth as brothers and sisters."[40] King wasn't anti-technology per se, but keenly understood how the arc of scientific progress could give the illusion that equivalent gains had been made in the social, cultural, political, and ecological realms. One can marvel at the technical capacities of the modern age while noting the leverage lost in other spheres.

Undoubtedly, not all technologies are equivalent nor do they fit neatly within a unitary analysis. Some technologies are widely considered beneficial, and it could exacerbate inequities to rein them in abruptly, as with certain medical advances or farming techniques. In this light, utilitarian perspectives can be invoked in considering whether on balance a particular technology does more good than harm, or a distributive frame can be deployed to inquire if the benefits and burdens are being managed in an egalitarian manner, or a teleological lens can be utilized in which the ends being sought can justify the means used to get there. Since modern lives increasingly are interconnected and dependent upon myriad technologies, the consequences of these choices within an emergent global web are being realized in the lives of individuals and communities everywhere. This suggests that decisions about appropriate technologies should be made at more proximate scales rather than by remote actors who often hold strong pecuniary interests.

Despite the relative lack of transparency associated with many emerging technologies, as well as the largely unaccounted nature of their potential negative impacts, they are remaking the map of our sociopolitical, economic, environmental, cultural, and even spiritual terrains in real-time. One need not be a scientist or scholar to grasp the impacts of smartphones and social media, or how sophisticated algorithms and artificial intelligences are impacting every sector from commerce and education to media and politics. With digital technologies pushing the envelope of speed and scale, as well as how multifariously people interface with them, the next frontier promises still greater transformations of virtual, augmented, and other forms of full-sensory experiences in a wider range of domains. In fact, many of these tools are touted as empathy-builders, as with virtual experiences of solitary confinement or 'natural' disasters.

Against this backdrop, the question of what constitutes a 'just technology' is not merely the province of policymakers and pundits. It is, rather, also about how people personally manage the technologies at their disposal, how they interact with and through them, how they choose to utilize them, and for what purposes. Social movements will use technology to organize and mobilize; teachers use technology to educate and inspire; community organizations use technology to network and convene. This article was written, produced, and distributed through myriad forms of technology. The food you eat likely was the result of technology, and the health outcomes you experience are as well. By now, the life of nearly every human on the planet is bound up with high technology—and the fate of the planet itself may depend on how we navigate this.

Given the moment of tech saturation in which we now find ourselves, it may come as a surprise that people have been thinking about these issues for far longer. The parable of *Frankenstein* coincides with numerous Transcendentalist literary figures warning about the rise of incipient methods of social control. As John Stuart Mill wrote in the early industrial era: "Supposing it were possible to get houses built, corn grown, battles fought, causes tried, and even churches erected and prayers said, by machinery—by automatons in human form—it would be a considerable loss to exchange for these automatons even the men and women who at present inhabit the more civilized parts of the world, and who assuredly are but starved specimens of what nature can and will produce."[41] Even further back, Plautus (c. 200 BC) lamented: "The gods confound the man who first found out how to distinguish hours, and confound him, too, who, in this place, set up a sundial to cut and hack my day so wretchedly into small pieces."[42]

This brief digression is not intended to be a comprehensive take on these complex issues. It is, instead, raised here in order to point out a number of flashpoints that can become chokepoints if left unattended. Specifically, we are confronted with the core question of whether the crises initiated by human enterprise and expansion can be remedied by more of the same. Can we ask the smartest AI we have to solve climate change—and if we do, might it declare that we are the problem? Likewise, as we consider the ramifications of reconnecting to and through place, it is imperative to inquire whether this sort of regrounding will yield enough bounty to provision the billions of inhabitants of this world, or whether some domain of technological megaproduction will remain necessary (and if so, how will those operations not swallow the small-scale ones)? We might imagine a future of peace and plenty, or at least one in which people are working to restore places and rectify patterns of degradation, but who will have the capacity to get there? Is the future inherently bound up with high-tech interventions, or will there be an equivalent sense of innovation at other scales and through additional means of reconnecting to the world?

ECOTOPIAN ASPIRATIONS

Following this trajectory, an opportunity emerged to facilitate a course on ecotopian literature in a maximum-security prison facility as part of a new credit-bearing college program. At first glance this might seem like an odd juxtaposition, but in practice the confluence makes perfect sense. If we are called to reimagine spaces by extending webs of interrelationships and reaffirming the centrality of thinking beyond the baseline of the world as we now find it, then places of relative isolation and even abandonment would be essential points in the grid. And if the people in those spaces can find connections to an expansive ecology through imaginative engagement and open-minded inquiry, then it seems conceivable wherever we may find ourselves. (Note that people there often are denied access to many technologies that others take for granted.) We may not have chosen our primary places, but there still are options for transforming them.

The course was designed as an extrapolation of one taught previously over many years in a more typical classroom environment, combining fictional and nonfictional accounts of ecotopian ideals with a range of assignments fostering analysis and creativity in equal parts. The first book we read together in the course was the novel *The Dispossessed,* written by Ursula K. Le Guin nearly half a century ago.[43] At its core, the book asks readers to consider how ideals and pragmatics converge in building a sustainable and just society. In Le Guin's imagined future there are nine "known worlds" populated by humans, with Earth itself represented as a post-apocalyptic Terra destroyed by greed and excess—but with our present Earth reflected through the fictional world of Urras with its capitalist, militaristic, classist societal structures. Le Guin holds up a mirror to both our fears and shortsightedness as well as our hopes and aspirations—sentiments epitomized by her 2014 acceptance speech of a National Book Foundation award:

> Hard times are coming, when we'll be wanting the voices of writers who can see alternatives to how we live now, can see through our fear-stricken society and its obsessive technologies to other ways of being, and even imagine real grounds for hope. We'll need writers who can remember freedom—poets, visionaries—realists of a larger reality.... We live in capitalism, its power seems inescapable—but then, so did the divine right of kings. Any human power can be resisted and changed by human beings. Resistance and change often begin in art. Very often in our art, the art of words.[44]

Through the journey of a central character (the physicist Shevek, from the anarchistic world Anarres) the novel explores the tensions between competing political and economic systems while confronting essential (even existential) questions of power, ideology, ecology, and human nature. Shevek's focus on temporality leads him to seek a bridge between worlds and to break down walls (literal and figurative) as he works to discern a complex integration of time as both sequential and simultaneous. The answer Shevek is seeking will have substantial impacts on communication, travel, and the possibilities of genuine interconnection among the known worlds—but reactionary interests also covet this knowledge for their own power and profit.

The narrative weaves an inherent ambiguity into the characters and the ultimate vision alike. As a scientist-philosopher working toward integrating dichotomies (in his case, the notions of time as unitary and unfolding), Shevek bridges worlds and theories in a way that provides a potential model for how a healthy society can be organized, with both oneness and infinitude as pillars. This critical nexus of maximal individual freedom with a strong sense of how all people (and everything, actually) are inherently interconnected is in fact the ethos of Shevek's home world of Anarres, even as he begins to see it drifting from its delicate yet durable ideals and activities. Ultimately the choice Shevek faces with the burden/gift of insight is squarely framed: is it more utopian to believe that a better world is possible, or that this one will turn out fine in the end?

Reconnecting with and through place through reinhabitation opens a space for various 'thought experiments' about designing a better world. Such experiences yield a sense that conducting a thought experiment is more than just a philosophical exercise. In a world where freedom is only selectively available, where visible and invisible walls pervade landscapes and serve to divide allegiances, there is value in freeing our minds to ponder other possibilities than those deemed viable by current constraints. If we could imagine a world of our own making, one that elegantly expresses both unity and diversity, what might it look like? How would such a world address the manifold crises that are destroying the world we have? These are eminently practical concerns, even as we may recognize that they find initial traction in the realm of ideas and imaginations. These sorts of core inquiries framed the classroom discussions around texts such as Le Guin's.

In *The Dispossessed,* the ideological founder of the ostensibly ecotopian world Anarres was a woman named Odo, who had a vision of a society grounded in the "rhythms of life on the planet."[45] Odo's foundational treatise was based on an ideal of "complex organicism" that sought to integrate "natural and social ecology" in a healthy, just, sustainable, and mutually reinforcing way.[46] This vision (titled *The Social Organism* by Odo, who perhaps serves as a stand-in for Le Guin herself) rejects all forms of waste (biophysical and sociological), dispenses with profit and power as the basic (or sole) motivators of human conduct, and grounds all of its processes in a "love of nature" that manifests by recognizing that humans are enmeshed in the web of life and the overall patterns evident in the cosmos.[47] In this, we are reminded that "ecology is all about relationships"[48]—both among ourselves and with our places and worlds.

This vision, however, was designed to be implemented and not just imagined—reflecting larger themes in Le Guin's work focusing on "relationships between ideas and material realities."[49] Odo was seeking to address a range of fundamental issues that imperiled human dignity, and even our very existence. As Le Guin suggests, Odo was imprisoned before society actually put her in a prison, living in an open-air colony of waste, toxicity, injustice, degradation (human and ecological), and routine violence—promising no future except a steady descent into brutality and, if unchecked, annihilation. Shevek himself ultimately (spoiler alert!) chooses to return to Anarres despite its creeping authoritarianism and clear dangers in doing so—in essence, to reinhabit his life and his home world. In the face of an unsustainable reality, the role of the visionary is to engage the structures that promulgate intensifying disasters, focusing on root causes rather than forever reacting to the symptoms and manifestations. Beyond that, those aspiring to ecotopian visions also must be ready to transcend structures that cannot change.

CONC(RETE) (AL)LUSIONS

The themes broached in *The Dispossessed* (and overall in the aforementioned course, in which we also read novels by Octavia Butler and Margaret Atwood, among other texts) hark back to the central question and the core challenge posed by this essay, namely: how can an ethos of reinhabitation and practices of placemaking combine with ecotopian aspirations to address structural issues in a world plagued by dire crises at all levels? A partial answer is provided by Shevek directly, during a conversation with a skeptic on Urras: "What is idealistic about social cooperation, mutual aid, when it is the only means of staying alive?"[50] A so-called thought experiment ceases to be mere theory and is no longer experimental when it offers a tangible basis for survival in a world where that cannot be taken for granted. Aspirations are crucial for this work, as people and communities strive to reweave the threads of their stories and habits of being wherever they are.

The aim, then, is not to cast about seeking a new world or idyllic vista or perfect narrative to (re)inhabit—it is, instead, to rekindle empathetic engagement with the people and places all around us, as we find them. In this, may what Singh refers to as "the world-destroying world-machine" be transformed into the seeds of "multiple, viable, alternative worlds"[51]—with all of us serving as levers of transformation: aware, embodied, freed from the constraints of linear time, imaginatively imbued with a repurposed epistemology of seeing and being, learning and yearning and healing and feeling as we go. The journey ahead simply may be to reclaim a vigorous sense of the "primeval connections to the ground beneath [us]," as Sofia Ahlberg suggests in *An Ecotopian Lexicon*.[52] Space may beckon, but place still remains full of wonders.

Bringing the inquiry full circle, the aim here has been to problematize the growing assertion that humankind must further separate itself from the vicissitudes of nature out of necessity. This argument is at best a form of misplaced adventurism and at worst a harbinger of human extinction. Nonetheless, it is to be taken seriously, not merely because it reflects the interests of powerful forces in society but due to its historical underpinnings as the basis of mechanistic thinking that has brought incredible progress for some and immiseration for others—and that is substantially impinging upon the planet's habitability for any of us. The appeal being advanced here is intended to upend that trajectory to nowhere by urging a deep reconnection with the places and people wherever we may be—indeed, *everywhere*—in order to forestall impending disaster and to galvanize solidarity. In this spirit may we reinhabit the world, and the world us.

RANDALL AMSTER, J.D., Ph.D., is Co-Director and Teaching Professor of Environmental Studies at Georgetown University. He teaches and publishes on subjects including peace and nonviolence, social and environmental justice, political theory, and emerging technologies. His most recent book is *Peace Ecology* (Routledge, 2014).

NOTES

1. Stephen Collis, *Once in Blockadia* (Vancouver, British Columbia: Talonbooks, 2016), 120.
2. Jennifer Kite-Powell, "A New Look at How Vertical Farming Can Help Decouple Food from Nature," *Forbes Magazine,* November 5, 2022. https://www.forbes.com /sites/jenniferhicks/2022/11/05/a-new-look-at-how-vertical-farming-can-help -decouple-food-from-nature/.
3. Kyle Bladow and Jennifer Ladino, eds., *Affective Ecocriticism: Emotion, Embodiment, Environment* (Lincoln: University of Nebraska Press, 2018), 2.
4. Alexa Weik von Mossner, *Affective Ecologies: Empathy, Emotion, and Environmental Narrative* (Columbus: The Ohio State University Press, 2017), 37.
5. Ibid., 38.
6. Irma Allen, "The Trouble with Rewilding . . ." *Undisciplined Environments,* December 14, 2016. https://undisciplinedenvironments.org/2016/12/14/the-trouble -with-rewilding/.
7. von Mossner, *Affective Ecologies,* 3.
8. Anna Lowenhaupt Tsing, *The Mushroom at the End of the World: On the Possibility of Life in Capitalist Ruins* (Princeton: Princeton University Press, 2015), 20.
9. Ernest Callenbach, "Epistle to the Ecotopians," *The Nation,* May 7, 2012. https:// www.thenation.com/article/archive/epistle-ecotopians/.
10. Robin Wall Kimmerer, *Braiding Sweetgrass: Indigenous Wisdom, Scientific Knowledge, and the Teachings of Plants* (Minneapolis: Milkweed Editions, 2015), 327.
11. Joshua Lockyer and James R. Veteto, eds., *Environmental Anthropology Engaging Ecotopia: Bioregionalism, Permaculture, and Ecovillages* (New York: Berghahn Books, 2013), 8.
12. Gary Snyder, "Reinhabitation," *Mānoa (Cascadia: The Life and Breath of the World)* 25, no. 1 (2013 [1976]): 44–48.
13. John Charles Ryan, "Humanity's Bioregional Places: Linking Space, Aesthetics, and the Ethics of Reinhabitation," *Humanities* 1, no. 1 (2012): 80–103, doi: 10.3390/h1010080.
14. Alexa Scully, "Decolonization, Reinhabitation and Reconciliation: Aboriginal and Place-Based Education," *Canadian Journal of Environmental Education* 17 (2012): 148–58.
15. Matthew Humphrey, "Reinhabiting Place: The Work of Bioregional Discipleship," *The Other Journal: An Intersection of Theology and Culture* 24 (2014): 1–15.
16. Devon G. Peña, "Endangered Landscapes and Disappearing Peoples? Identity, Place, and Community in Ecological Politics," in *The Environmental Justice Reader: Politics, Poetics, and Pedagogy,* eds. Joni Adamson, Mei Mei Evans, and Rachel Stein (Tucson: The University of Arizona Press, 2002), 61, 72.
17. Sylvia Rodríguez, *Acequia: Water Sharing, Sanctity, and Place* (Santa Fe, NM: School for Advanced Research Press, 2006), 80.
18. Ibid.
19. Peña, "Endangered Landscapes," 75.
20. Lawrence Buell, *Writing for an Endangered World: Literature, Culture, and Environment in the U.S. and Beyond* (Cambridge: Harvard University Press, 2003), 84.
21. von Mossner, *Affective Ecologies,* 171.
22. Tsing, *The Mushroom at the End of the World,* 19.

23. Kimberly Skye Richards, "Solastalgia," in *An Ecotopian Lexicon,* eds. Matthew Schneider-Mayerson and Brent Ryan Bellamy (Minneapolis: University of Minnesota Press, 2019), 268.

24. Ibid., 269.

25. Ibid., 272.

26. von Mossner, *Affective Ecologies,* 174.

27. Grace Lee Boggs, "The Beloved Community of Martin Luther King," *YES!,* May 21, 2004. https://www.yesmagazine.org/issue/hope-conspiracy/2004/05/21/the -beloved-community-of-martin-luther-king.

28. von Mossner, *Affective Ecologies,* 187.

29. Vandana Singh, *Utopias of the Third Kind* (Oakland, Calif.: PM Press, 2022), 33.

30. Ibid., 35.

31. Christine E. Nieves Rodriguez, "Community Is Our Best Chance," in *All We Can Save: Truth, Courage, and Solutions for the Climate Crisis,* eds. Ayana Elizabeth Johnson and Katharine K. Wilkinson (New York: One World, 2020), 366.

32. Aldo Leopold, "The Land Ethic," in *A Sand County Almanac* (New York: Ballantine, 1970 [1949]), 237–264.

33. Ibid., 253.

34. Jane Zelikova, "Solutions Underfoot," in *All We Can Save: Truth, Courage, and Solutions for the Climate Crisis,* eds. Ayana Elizabeth Johnson and Katharine K. Wilkinson (New York: One World, 2020), 288.

35. Ibid., 289.

36. Leah Penniman, "Black Gold," in *All We Can Save: Truth, Courage, and Solutions for the Climate Crisis,* eds. Ayana Elizabeth Johnson and Katharine K. Wilkinson (New York: One World, 2020), 303, 309.

37. Damayanti Banergee, "Just Places: Creating a Space for Place in Environmental Justice," *Societies Without Borders* 7, no. 2 (2012): 169–91.

38. Will Steffen, et al., "Planetary Boundaries: Guiding Human Development on a Changing Planet," *Science,* January 15, 2015.

39. Kendra Pierre-Louis, "Wakanda Doesn't Have Suburbs," in *All We Can Save: Truth, Courage, and Solutions for the Climate Crisis,* eds. Ayana Elizabeth Johnson and Katharine K. Wilkinson (New York: One World, 2020), 139.

40. Martin Luther King, Jr. (speech, n.d.), https://www.youtube.com/watch?v= kTC3cieV_NA.

41. John Stuart Mill, *On Liberty* (1859).

42. Plautus (poem, n.d.), https://www.laphamsquarterly.org/time/hacked-days.

43. Ursula K. Le Guin, *The Dispossessed: An Ambiguous Utopia* (New York: Harper, 1974).

44. Ursula K. Le Guin (speech, National Book Foundation, November 19, 2014), https:// www.ursulakleguin.com/nbf-medal.

45. Le Guin, *The Dispossessed,* 233.

46. Ibid., 95–96.

47. Ibid., 185.

48. Zelikova, "Solutions Underfoot," 287.

49. Michael Horka, "Heyiya," in *An Ecotopian Lexicon,* eds. Matthew Schneider-Mayerson and Brent Ryan Bellamy (Minneapolis: University of Minnesota Press, 2019), 103.

50. Le Guin, *The Dispossessed*, 135.

51. Singh, *Utopias of the Third Kind*, 35.

52. Sofia Ahlberg, "Fotminne," in *An Ecotopian Lexicon*, eds. Matthew Schneider-Mayerson and Brent Ryan Bellamy (Minneapolis: University of Minnesota Press, 2019), 63.

Wild Design

Gambiarra, Complexity and Responsibility

MONAÍ DE PAULA ANTUNES

Abstract

This paper proposes different approaches to design, referring to gambiarra practices and artifacts and their relation to complexity theory, evoking critical theorists that take undecidability into account in order to link gambiarra to operations that breed complexity and responsibility. The word gambiarra comes from Brazilian slang and describes an intervention or artifact meant to provide a provisory solution to an unexpected event or crisis. This kind of alternative design differs radically from conventional design because it does not come from formally trained, engineer-minded, projects. Instead, it lacks control, stability and durability. As it offers no permanent solution, it opens room for further accidents and is messy, especially if compared to a conservative model for creation that praises human predominance, soundness and efficiency. Therefore, gambiarra often has negative connotations that this analysis aims to challenge, by relating it to principles of complexity theory. Complexity theory is a transdisciplinary field for research aimed at the organization of living systems, with a vast understanding of networks and what life and govern are. It gathers insights from different disciplines to explore the interconnectivity between individuals, their systems and environment. It unveils how ambivalent information/noise relationships are fundamental for the increase of diversity in a system. It also displays the intelligent dynamics resulting from seemingly insignificant neighborhood relations that collectively make it possible to adapt and continuously change structures. With that in mind, the "deficient" aspect of gambiarra becomes more valuable, as it hints at a potential to generate new information and structures beyond entropic models that perpetuate the same logics across time. Michel Serres's information theory presented in the book The Parasite *is brought up in comparison to gambiarra, in order to explore the potential of interdependent ambiguous relationships that may not fit in dominant forms of discourse. Concomitantly, Vilém Flusser's notion of responsibility reinforces the argument that a fabric of dynamic differences can emerge out of mutual engagement and indeterminacy. Underlying, this paper concerns with drafting ecological discourses and practices that can embrace contradictions and the plurality of worlds, noticing complex phenomena that have been pushed to the margins, while also decentralizing from hegemonic models. It questions the predominance of the prevailing design paradigm in the search for non-eurocentric and non-anthropocentric human-environment relationships and forms of provision of human needs.*

INTRODUCTION

The words "wild" and "design" carry with them sustaining human dichotomies. The combination of both releases a wide array of conflicts and contradictions. "Wild" can't escape eurocentric traditions of naturalism and supremacy, "design"—often untranslated from english—takes for granted human domineering agency over processes. This research embraces the irony and contradictions of its title, interested in design practices in which human agency is not driven by notions of control, stability, durability or safety, instead they resonate with synonyms of "wild", such as untamed, radical, marginal, uncontrollable, uncivilized, informal, undisciplined, unruly and unconventional. It sees supremacist logics in realms way more discreet than neo-Nazi rallies, for example, in our overall understanding of design. As design is a pivot of how humans provide for their needs and solve their problems, this research calls attention to the ways in which it suppresses everything "off-the-grid" and by doing so, becomes unresponsive to circumstances, namely, to the environment.

Gambiarra is the starting point of this research—the first section of this paper is dedicated to a careful definition, including academic and artistic research that have been conducted around the topic. In addition, we also present some considerations about *favelas* in their material-discursive similarities to *gambiarra*, as adaptive and marginalized residential areas, shaping our view of them as organisms and organizations.

The second part of the article is dedicated to a brief presentation of Complexity Theory, which provides a more suitable scientific framework to support the understanding of *gambiarra*. Observing the *strange loops* present in complex adaptive systems through the incessant relationship between noise and information, we head towards Michel Serres's information theory elaborated in "The Parasite" to bring undecidability to the argumentative field. This notion is key to understanding *gambiarra* in negentropic terms, as a design practice that creates new information and breeds diversity and complexity, an open system in dialogue with the environment.

The third section of the paper considers the notion of undecidability alongside Vilém Flusser's responsibility underlying a draft for non-conservative design and ecological thinking based upon *gambiarra*—or further, Wild Design—which is able to radically embrace contradiction, and by doing so, transcend binaries beyond philosophical terms.

GAMBIARRA AND DESIGN THINKING

Gambiarra is a Brazilian term related to an artifact or practice, and refers to an improvised immediate solution for an unexpected event. It's often regarded as a sloppy approach to engineering and problem-solving and is commonly related to the way of life of underprivileged spheres of Brazilian society. It may have a positive connotation, however, as a form of intrinsic improvisation know-how that Brazilians use for adapting and taking the best out of critical situations. Thus, such strategies oscillate between cleverly finding unconventional paths within the formal system and actually violating the norm of conduct.

A *gambiarra* may or may not last—it can collapse, demand constant maintenance or evolve into something else, among other possibilities. For example, a chair leg that breaks and is replaced by a wooden stick from a discarded broom. Or in actual off-grid neighborhoods—whether deprived of public electricity supply or when inhabitants simply cannot afford the utility—where energy is stolen from the public network by intercepting wires directly at the street's power transformer. Such adjustments are done one by one, gradually altering the planned urban landscape into an illegal, unreliable, unpredictable and often dangerous mesh.

Gambiarra is untamed. Starting from an unexpected situation and/or based on an instantaneous insight, it is a process that spontaneously creates something that allows for building an artifact in a way

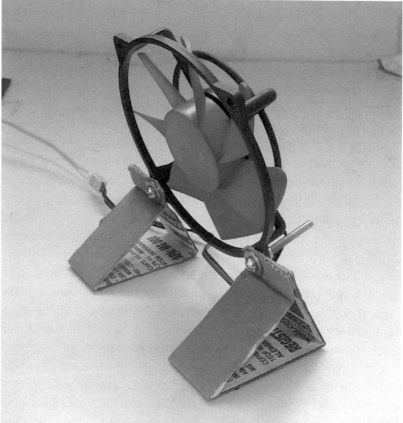

Figures 1 & 2. Examples of gambiarra. Image credits: Monai de Paula Antunes.

that improves its current function, inspired by a particular need or disposable material resource. *Gambiarra* is not a method, it is a constant resistance to method. At the same time, it is a necessity. Contrarily, engineering, design, urban planning, architecture, informatics, and to a certain extent, even art, are often based on control, safety, security, efficiency, productivity, predictability, certainty about outcomes and revenues, straightforwardness, minimalism, functionality, precision, definiteness. These principles, opposite to what *gambiarra* represents, are some of the most valuable features in the realm of design, if not indispensable in all design practices.

Despite its association with defective or overly disordered conceptions, *gambiarra* is used as an allegory by different researchers and artists envisioning an alternative approach to design. It has been an illustrious icon of the DIY and upcycling movement, and since the 2000s has been appropriated widely by Brazilian media art and media activism, having reached the realms of academic research. Rodrigo Boufleur compares *gambiarra* to industrial design, finding similarities between these in terms of intent, and differences in terms of social context. The author also points to their intertwinement, stating that *gambiarra* "emerges at the limits and impacts provided by the industrial model of production and consumption."[1] Boufleur presents different examples of how *gambiarra* can be inclusive, whether by harnessing waste as raw material or by adapting objects to specific and special needs, e.g. for and by people with unique (dis)abilities and without access to sophisticated technology. In addition, he points out *gambiarra* as a sustainable approach in the context of post-industrial design, which complements artifacts produced in a capitalist industrial mode while subverting their design. The work of Michel de Certeau is in line with this approach, as his notions of *everyday practices* and *production through consumption* support Boufleur's theory of *gambiarra* as a "permanent manifestation of human creativity and social tactics able to maneuver the traditional order of market-based perspective of passive consumption."[2]

Gambiologia, "the science of *gambiarra*", is a Brazilian art collective that proposes a dialogue between the Brazilian tradition of improvisation and electronic art.[3] Through the promotion of workshops with different non-specialized communities, urban interventions, debates and exhibitions, their work is mainly a strategy for critical and creative

Figure 3. A Armadura Gambiológica—Relógio (The gambiological armor—Watch), artwork by Gambiologia. Image credits: Daniel Mansur

reinvention of obsolete devices and media. They approach the interchange between contemporary and folk art forms through openness and informality during interactions between the artists, the public, and objects. Beyond the common sense of recycling, their notion of reuse is an expressive resource to construct artworks with/in excessive waste. By working with "low-technology" and collecting with the intent of transforming the resulting collection, the group's works engage with critical thinking on accumulation and appropriation, proposing a re-signification of disposed objects and praising the hacker culture for its system-subversive practices.[4]

In turn, Fernanda Bruno explores *gambiarra*'s shamelessness and inventiveness in dialogue with cognitive and political potentialities, as formulated by Gilbert Simondon.[5] The object—as conceived in a conventional design paradigm—is understood and acquired as an entity complete in itself, segregated from designer and consumer. Despite the proximity during development and usage, human action does not find points of insertion in this closed system. In Bruno's work, such integrity is perverted by *gambiarra*'s audacity, open ends and matter-of-factness—not only in visual terms, but cognitively, unveiling and unsilencing entire sociotechnical heterogeneous networks of human and non-human agencies that produce and maintain objects, as well as the agency of objects themselves, simultaneously actors and affects. 'Gambiarra operates in a regime of "open knowledge" in its own materiality; from its origin passing through its assembly and uses, it is based on a common, shared and collective knowledge that builds itself.'[6] In this way, it goes against the process of an encapsulation of the network of actors and mediations necessary for the production and maintenance of technical entities, opposing the tendency of consolidation of technical objects into black boxes, as formulated by Bruno Latour,[7] and similarly, by Vilém Flusser.[8]

Further into other materialities and geopolitical contexts, in "Gambiarra and Sound Experimentalism", a doctoral thesis by Giuliano Obici, Brazilian material and technical culture meet music and sound art. In this research, *gambiarra* is thought together with the design of new musical instruments and sound art practices, under the light of improvisation, utilitarian readjustment, subversion of industrial design, reverse engineering, risk and instability of an object's usability, and technological disobedience.[9] The latter, which plays a fundamental role in Obici's argument, is an important part of the work of Cuban artist and designer Ernesto Oroza.

Oroza elaborates on the theory of an "architecture of necessity", which, in the case of Cuba, owes mainly to the country's political regime and the US-American embargo. Oroza's disobedience holds a relation to Thoreau's civil disobedience, but in the Cuban example disrespect is manifested towards the authority of technology and the sense of identity and inflexibility of Western objects. For both Obici and Oroza, as for many authors interested in decolonizing technology, subversion and the pursuit of autonomy are crucial in a technological context where components are rarely designed from scratch and are imported from different production and consumption realities. These rigid topologies, with their embedded biases, perpetuate a logic of exploitation and oppression, as they impose a network of modes of being and relating. In the words of Obici: "In this context, *gambiarra* can be seen as an emergent behavior in this ecosystem, and it deals with unconventional solutions, covering a spectrum of applications and uses related to the context of a culture mediated by technology."[10]

Figure 4. Two Wall Clocks, artwork by Ernesto Oroza. Image credits: Ernesto Oroza

As evidenced by the previous approaches, *gambiarra* highlights the material culture of our times—whether by exposing excessive modes of production and consumption, disjointed from our socio-environmental reality and deaf to local needs and participation, or by featuring adaptation, users' intervention and the rejection of the notion of waste, turned into material resources.[11] Across the scope of these examples, *gambiarra* suggests a "way to accomplish something by circumventing or bending the rules or social conventions."[12] Moreover, as an object, *gambiarra* is in action, in transit, in transition—a *gambiarra-process*[13] moves away from separations between nature, culture and technology and their correlated mechanisms of alienation. On the other hand, it moves towards the gesture: ". . . *gambiarra* does not materialize in objects, but resides in the very fugacity of the gesture. . . . The practice of *gambiarra* rearranges not only the materials of everyday life, but also the very *distribution of the sensible*, the fixed places for each body, the uses for each product, the already codified ways of operating."[14]

The political dimension of *gambiarra* reaches the far end of networks of influence in everyday politics through a non-technocratic, somewhat artistic experience that emancipates by inventing new practices, transforming noise into speech—it represents a tangible manifestation of other modes of doing, a liberating realization. "By returning uncertainty to the world, *gambiarra* makes it possible to indicate that other worlds are possible. The questioning of naturality revitalizes the power to produce something new."[15]

GAMBIARRA NETWORKS

The complex of Brazilian *favelas* exemplifies how *gambiarra* can evolve into an entity, i.e. a network of influences exposed through a sequence of *gambiarras* both on the level of design and materiality and in terms of human communication and organization. Vibrant and complex organizations are revealed in Janice Perlman's experiences with different characters and scenarios of *favela* settlements in Rio between 1969 and 2009, "where the unexpected is expected and spontaneity is norm."[16] She provokes a "paradigm shift away from perceiving the urban poor as "marginal" or irrelevant to the system to seeing them as tightly integrated into the system, albeit in a perversely asymmetrical fashion."[17] These environments are presented as symbiotic, self-regulated systems, with no gaps and little to do with the legal and bureaucratic frames of the city, where communities are humanly welcoming and people take care of each other. Negotiations take place all the time, and by means of continuous confrontation and adjustments, people from different backgrounds and ethnicities, with different interests and lifestyles, come together to overcome their critical situations. Characters are portrayed as clever, determined, resourceful, energetic; as resilient people taking responsibility for their ambitions, and most importantly, for their everyday livelihood, where certain issues are taken care of collectively. Furthermore, people trying to establish themselves in such areas seem to be deeply engaged in understanding and playing along with the unsteady orders of these communities.[18]

Historically, these settlements were mostly occupied by migrants coming from remote places around Brazil's rural areas, some of which were small villages organized "in a kind of primitive communism, with no political leader and with everyone sharing equally when the fishing boats returned with the catch of the day."[19] Technological transitions—- e.g. communication media such as the radio, which brought news from the capital and of lives elsewhere—have changed villagers' interests and aspirations. Gradually, a massive national migration took place towards Rio de Janeiro and São Paulo, mainly from the Northeast of the country, where the semi-arid climate and poverty caused starvation and high mortality rates. Although the first *favela* dates back to 1897, they were not consolidated before the period between the 1930's and 1960's. By then, the State had already been undertaking considerable efforts to displace *favela* residents—considered by the city's urban planning as a cluster of second-rate people and diseases displaying an ungraceful aesthetic. After families were removed to the outskirts, Brazil's "economic miracle" in the late 1960's flooded urban centers with rural migrants, when the *favelas* were reoccupied by the new incomers.

In large cities like Rio de Janeiro, where hills alternate with flat areas, the rich and middle class neighborhoods occupied the flat areas, as did the city center and administration, whereas the hillside was seen as too dangerous to build on, for its topography and climate as well as its military vulnerability. Thus, due to their proximity to the economic area of the city, migrants took advantage of the undesired land to grow the *favelas*, harnessing this spot of connection to where money flowed and could be made. Providing services, mainly unqualified labor force, dealing with scrap, receiving charity, smuggling . . . the location of the *favelas* gave poor people uphill access to the crumbs of the city's table.

With regard to design, 'they could be seen as precursors of the "new urbanism" with their high-density, low-rise architecture, featuring façades variously angled to catch a breeze or a view, and shade trees and shutters to keep them cool. The building materials were construction-site discards and scraps, the so-called "recycled materials" of today. They were owner-designed, built, and occupied, and followed the organic curves of the hillsides rather than a rigid grid-pattern.[20] Construction techniques varied from rustic natural building methods, such as earthen plaster, cob, wattle and daub, to wasteful uses of cement and beams in the absence of formal engineering knowledge. The building process was often slow or never-ending—according to the time it takes to save up for materials and to build gradually, often decades. Land ownership has been mostly off-topic; in the course of a century, only a small number of *favela* inhabitants had been officially conceded property of their housing. In short, as Perlman herself states, "[t]he concept of the house as a thing or a commodity began to give way to the concept of housing as a verb, a process."[21]

House as a process is also a concept applied not only to the material and building strategies present in the *favela*, but to a larger definition of *house* interdependent and co-autonomous to a *configuration of houses*.[22] "The house is not only a transmissible individual property, a thing, a family property, an ideology. It is a practice, a strategic construction in the production of domesticity. Neither is it an isolated, self-contained entity. The house only exists in the context of a network of domestic unity. It is thought and experiences in interrelation with other houses that participate in its construction—in the symbolic and concrete sense."[23] In practice, this position of a house in relation to others, as well as the *mutability of the houses*, manifests for example in the kitchen, where often members of other houses have their regular meals in someone else's kitchen (children and grandchildren eating daily at the grandmother's kitchen).[24] People's life's narrations are punctuated by the transformations made to their houses, which also points to the forms in which houses are processually divided or multiplied as offshoots of previous houses for circumstantial (i.e. birth, death) or economical reasons. The new houses remain materially and/or symbolically linked to the previous ones, sometimes even outside of *favelas*, connected to a primary house in the rural provenance. How houses are built is public knowledge, composing a collective narrative about the past and an imagination of the future, in which "the material house is one of the elements of a complex arrangement of relations that include people and objects. This "arrangement and their elements are mutually constituted in the circulations and transformations—in motion."[25]

Narratives about the *favelas* have been strongly politically ressigni-fied by activists in the last decades, gradually bound to new interpre-tative possibilities in the antiracists struggles in Brazil. The encounter between *favela* social movements and antiracist movements takes place in the fight against state, namely, police brutality, which is clearly displayed in the space of the favelas as a racist violence. The process of destigmatization of *favelas* walks side with its situated-ness as the centers of politicized Brazilian blackness, as the *hashtag* *#vidasnafavelaimportam* [Lifes in the *favela* matter] alludes, translating black lives to a racial violence that embodied at the most in the place of *favelas*.[26] The ways in which the *favela* is positively presented today is related rather to a narrative of resistance and racialization than of har-mony, against both its criminalization but also its romanticization.[27]

The recurring accidents, such as landslides during the rainy season, as well as fatalities, repression or any other of the innumerous forces that could unexpectedly provoke disproportionate events in the favelas, perpetuate a liminal state that is exacerbated by the combination of a susceptible and non-arbitrary system and the marginalizing pressures upon it. The ceaseless handling of situations in which changing circum-stances prevail over predetermined architectures establishes an evolv-ing know-how on resolution, adaptation and reconfiguration. Through these continuous unfoldings, the bigger picture reveals an intelligent communication independent from a deliberately designed structure.

It must be noted that this view, far from being meant as a romantici-zation and aestheticization of the long-lasting and unjust sufferings of large portions of the population living and purposely placed in precar-ious conditions across time, aims to pay respect to the situated knowl-edges and skills in conviviality, communication and technology that are commonly overlooked and intentionally neglected, pointing to them as an example of dynamism and adaptability in times of apocalyptic anx-iety. As with *gambiarra*, in *favelas* extraordinary solutions emerge out of shortage, and in unexpected situations, or unplanned terrain, things are seen as potential assets. However, although this spontaneous de-sign considers accidents and admits events, it is inconsequential. It often generates other problems, which provide the necessary openness for unprecedented momentary results, for the new. At the same time that it embraces reuse and adaptation, it challenges an idealized view of environmentalism, as it does not take account of catastrophes and undesired outcomes.

The modes of communication between technology, matter, objects, humans and other entities in these systems might reveal structures that are more accommodating of circumstances than common practices in democratic state governance and environmental approaches based on control, protocol, dualism and technocracy. In the examples presented so far, human agency and dialogue with others favor immediate circumstances, as opposed to a conventionally pre-established structure. Due to their marginalized place in society, *gambiarra* and *favelas* and its constituting layers of entities evolve co-autonomously through negotiations and interactions that bypass a strict model for design, urbanization and human communication. The neighbor-to-neighbor conflict resolution is possible because of a *modus operandi* that values adaptation rather than a strict code of conduct. This makes *gambiarra* an off-grid structure where humans are in constant dialogue with each other and with events, technology, materials and the environment. As such, it allows room for momentum and maneuvers among different entities, compared to a predetermined architecture where safety and control are assured by strict functioning and rules. Furthermore, the promptness to answer to adversity, in other words, noise, in a way that incorporates the unexpected environmental interference into a new model, generates new information. That reveals how off-grid structures are living entities, namely ecosystems, while grid-like structures tend to perpetuate sameness and thus are moving towards entropy.

Rather than overlooking the injustices involved in a *gambiarra* framework, Wild Design is interested in offering a contribution to an ecological approach which questions environmentalist discourses that disregards certain features of the systemic intertwinement of the world, perpetuating the model underlying such injustices. From this viewpoint, let us consider that life on the edges might be maintained as distortedly rough precisely because it remains marginal to a system of supremacy often unwittingly ubiquitous, present in so many spheres of life, including design. *Gambiarra* is wild and requires the development of a frame of research that does not inadvertently tame it in time, an ecological language towards overcoming the dichotomies that persistently sustain all kinds of oppression: "Neither totalizing structures that repress differences nor oppositional differences that exclude commonality are adequate to the plurality of the world, the diversity upon which creative and productive life depends on."[28]

COMPLEXITY THEORY AND THE PARASITE: FROM UNDECIABILITY TO CREATIVE INTERACTION

Complexity Theory studies complex adaptive systems, which are systems able to reconfigure their patterns through their relations within and with their environment. It is a transdisciplinary field that mediates thought in biology, mathematics, information theory and computation, cybernetics, psychology, cognition and consciousness, art, design, architecture and technology, economy; catastrophe, process, chaos and game theory; quantum physics, neurosciences, communication, thermodynamics, genetics, philosophy, media theory and network culture, among others.

Complex adaptive systems can be found in very different contexts. They operate upon sets of patterns, which is to say that their behavior is not random or chaotic, but coordinated by accessible and known rules that are performed by every element of the system, resulting from the interaction of elements with themselves, their neighbors and environment. The main feature of such systems is that they are able to reconfigure their own rules, and they do so after a learning process that involves a collective memory, which reveals mnemonic ecologies. Examples vary from the stock market to a developing embryo.

Such systems are open networks that also relate to other systems. All sets follow certain patterns of behavior, a certain functioning. Through the interactions experienced and by processing information, the schemata reconfigures itself over time. Together, the interactions of the system consolidate a non-centralized intelligence, which recognizes patterns in itself and in the environment, stores knowledge on the history of internal/external patterns, and by doing so, is able to predict future events, reforming its own patterns based on these predictions and therefore feeding the memory of the system with past and future events.[29]

Properties of emergence—the process whereby larger entities arise through interactions among smaller or simpler entities—are recognized as the main principle for co-autonomous self-organization in adaptive systems. Emergence is the form in which immediate reactions to circumstances lived by individuals in a network, whether by themselves or with neighbors or the environment, generate a greater intelligence, non-totalizing by nature and in the absence of a centralizing power, acting as a whole. For instance, in an ant colony the queen does not give direct orders and does not tell the ants what to do; instead, each ant reacts to stimuli in the form of chemical scent from larvae, other ants, intruders, food and waste build-up, and leaves behind a chemical trail, which, in turn, provides a stimulus to other ants. In their system, each ant is an autonomous unit that reacts depending only on its local environment and the genetically encoded rules for its variety of ant. It is worth noting that genetics plays a role in this complex functioning, but it does not rule over the other interactions. In fact, information and its transmission take very different forms, entangled material and immaterial forms, within a structure that is non-linear, open and dynamic. This collective intelligence and communication model is based primarily on immediate careless responses, lacking centralized decision-making.

Complex adaptive systems are dynamic networks of interactions and relationships, not aggregations of static entities. They are adaptive in that their individual and collective behavior changes as a result of experience. These systems are neither programmed nor designed, but their development can be directed by the assembly of common experiences, as they are products of progressive adaptations. Progress in this context is measured by an increase in diversity and, correlatively, growth in complexity.

In such networks, circuits are recursive and reflexive yet not closed, unfolding from and folding back upon themselves, neither as final structures nor as a complete whole. *Strange loops* (Gödel) are self-reflexive circuits, which, although appearing to be circular, remain paradoxically open and generate *undecidability*. In the strange loops of these systems, complexity breeds diversity, which increases complexity, which breeds diversity on the one hand, system and environment are joint recursive circuits that create both unexpected and disproportionate changes; on the other hand, the openness of complex adaptive systems leads to aleatory changes in schemata that distinguish the point of departure from the point of arrival. This is the reason why complex adaptive systems must be co-adaptive: they adapt to systems that are adapting to them. Such co-adaptation compounds the complexity of the systems involved, every complex system is folded into more or less extensive networks of other complex systems.[30]

In *The Parasite*, Michel Serres elaborates on a description of systems based on the complexity that emerges from strange loops and undecidability. Serres celebrates an information theory that elegantly and radically traces some modes through which new information takes shape by means of reversal, interdependency and appropriation. *The Parasite* is a lyrical study on unsettling undecidable identities that cannot be reduced and that implicate paralogics: information and noise switch roles processually, reverberating their forms in increasingly complex loops. For Serres, noise is a sign of an increase in complexity. For those who can bear neither ambiguity or uncertainty, such noise must be eliminated; for those daring a more complex operation, however, noise is a welcome guest whose interruptions and disruptions are as creative as they are destructive.

> At the feast everyone is talking. At the door of the room there is a ringing noise, the telephone. Communication cuts conversation, the noise interrupting the messages. As soon as I start to talk with this new interlocutor, the sounds of the banquet become noise for the new "us." The system has shifted. If I approach the table, the noise slowly becomes conversation. In the system, noise and message exchange roles according to the position of the observer and the action of the actor, but they are transformed into one another as well as a function of time and of the system. They make order or disorder.[31]

The Parasite evokes plural, non-dualistic subjects under characters such as farm rats, city rats, the farmer (who turns out to be a tax farmer, living from the production of other farmers); a constant exchange of roles between who is the host, who is the guest, who is hospitable and who is hostile. The role of the parasite is eventually incorporated by all those once thought to be innocent, opening up an important shift in interpretations of systems held back by the paradoxes of binary thinking. The parasite is an operation, not a static entity; it is thus the joker, one of the characters that welcomes the step into multidimensionality. The joker is a relation, a *"liaison* agent" in dialogue with the material world. It has no *a priori* value established by convention, but only by social agreement. Yet it responds to circumstances, to the supernatural, to the environment:

> That joker is a logical object that is both indispensable and fascinating. Placed in the middle or at the end of a series, a series that has a law of order, it permits to bifurcate, to take another appearance, another direction, another order. The only describable difference between a method and a bricolage is the joker. The principle of bricolage is to make something by means of something else, a mash with a match-stick, a chicken wing with tissue meant for the thigh, and so forth. Just as the most general model of method is game, the good model for what is deceptively called bricolage is the joker.[32]

The Parasite drafts a theorem of ambiguity, back and forth between information and noise. Much like *gambiarra*, it prizes ambivalence as fundamental for the emergence of the new, ergo, of life. The parasite is the trickster with no fixed identity and no moral stiffness. It knows no waste, no form, no exteriority. It exposes the dynamism of systems, of boundaries and negotiations. Moreover, it acclaims characters that hold intrinsic negative connotations and makes amends by revealing their true generative qualities. As Hillis Miller elucidates the meaning of the prefix of its name:

> Para is a double antithetical prefix signifying at once proximity and distance, similarity and difference, interiority and exteriority, some-thing inside a domestic economy and at the same time outside it, something simultaneously this side of a boundary line, threshold or margin, and also beyond it . . . A thing "para", moreover, is not only simultaneously on both sides of the boundary line between inside and out. It is also the boundary itself, the screen, which is a permeable membrane connecting inside and outside. It confuses them with one another, allowing the outside in, making the inside out, dividing them and joining them. It also forms an ambiguous transition between one and the other.[33]

Like Serres, Hillis Miller sees great value in ambiguity. Moreover, it seems that ambiguity is precisely the operation that creates life, regulates order within chaos and *vice versa*.

> The parasite invents something new. He obtains energy and pays for it in information. He obtains the roast and pays for it in stories. Two ways of writing the new contract. He establishes an unjust pact; relative to the old type of balance, he builds a new one. He speaks in a logic considered irrational up to now, a new epistemology and a new theory of equilibrium. He makes the order of things as well as the states of things solid and gas into diagonals. He evaluates information. Even better: he discovers information in his voice and good words; he discovers the Spirit in the wind and the breath of air. He invents cybernetics.[34]

Observing the relationality of *gambiarra*, similar to what Serres suggests with the parasite, we are taken to question our ideas of what intelligence and governance are, and above all, what life is. Cybernetics is a transdisciplinary approach for exploring regulatory systems. The word comes from Greek and means "governance," explaining its direct relation to artificial ("non-human") intelligence. Despite the common association between cybernetics and virtuality or robotics, especially since the rise of the Internet and the development of "smart" technologies, cybernetics fundamentally deals with entities that do not correspond to a conventional understanding of what living is. It seeks life in patterns that do not necessarily take shape according to the strict biological definition of an organism—an organic living system that functions as an individual entity—yet they have influence and are influenced by ourselves and our social systems, having strong biopolitical implications.

The first order of cybernetics was concerned with developing control mechanisms designed to automatically follow a predetermined sequence of operations or respond to predetermined instructions. It carried a very stiff understanding of intelligence and was replaced by the second order of cybernetics—a foundation for systemic thinking—headed by thinkers such as Heinz von Foester, Margaret Mead, Gregory Bateson, Humberto Maturana and Francisco Varela. This take on cybernetics opened the door to understanding systems ecologically, regardless of the biological, informational or psychological nature of systems, for example. In recent decades, many discourses emerged from the intersection between cybernetics and ecology.[35] Such "new ecologies" concern different theories within several fields that reject dualism and binaries such as subject/object, interiority/exteriority, virtual/physical and fundamentally place ontology on relation, rather than on any individual entity: a series of different perspectives where relations rise above individuals and therefore everything that is living, every identity and every consciousness, is a result of an interaction, responds—i.e. feeds back—and is intertwined.

Although we aim to demonstrate a correlation of design and society with complexity and cybernetics in terms of how immediate actions lead to greater degrees of intelligence, it is worth noting that self-organization does not occur as a natural consequence of acting upon individual needs, nor relates to a sense of "harmony." It is very important to distinguish acting upon self-seeking interests and acting upon relations. Among other things, here *gambiarra* serves the purpose of illustrating an open circuit where boundaries between actors are porous and therefore the idea of individual, separate entities does not apply and neither does it foster interaction/progress. Contrarily, it is believed that self-organization emerges from co-autonomy, from engaging with one's neighbors, the dynamic order that evolves from dialogue. A social fabric that we can actually lean on emerges from constant adjustment between ourselves, our neighbors and our environment, from engagement and the responsibility that results from interaction, rather than from good intentions.

WILD DESIGN AND RESPONSIBILITY

> *Something is happening which doesn't necessarily have to do with the apparent central questions, and it's happening in the margins, in the ecological. We must come up with unexpected politics, alliances that we haven't thought of before. Undo identities and build a new space for them.*[36]

Wild Design is a framework evolving from the insights brought about by *gambiarra* but expanding into any design practice in which human agency comes through not as formal engineering processes, but dynamically develops into, as well as together with, systems. It takes into account design practices not driven by notions of control, stability, durability and safety, instead resonating with synonyms of wildness, such as untamed, radical, marginal, uncontrollable, uncivilized, informal, undisciplined, unruly and unconventional. In spirit, this framework is thought to accommodate human regulatory roles that are dialogical and process-oriented, i.e. human participation in creation and problem-solving that operates within a paradigm of intertwined and evolving architectures. Different from cultures in which humans fulfill their needs by anticipating, starting from scratch, conceiving, planning and executing every step of a process up to its final goal, Wild Design embraces concepts of design and technology that admit active participation of non-human agents in horizontal ways. Besides incorporating other modes of thinking about human design and communication within processes, this framework intends to contribute to the complex phenomena involved in the *arts of noticing*[37] that have long been placed peripherally in scientific, artistic, technological and social discourses.

This research began over ten years before its publication and, since its inception, criticizing the pretensions of democratic states and beliefs about their structures has become dicey. Wild Design fundamentally advocates for decentralization and against the insistence that bureaucracy—as firmly cemented in streamlined procedures—can lead to justice. However, we find ourselves in a moment in which centralized power takes new shapes, diffusing itself in foggy clouds. This suggests a process of dispersion, but in fact it strengthens supremacist logics and a centralized social apparatus as new shapes that are potentially harder to circumvent, with little or no foundation on a generally acceptable path towards a common good. In the midst of an ongoing information revolution topped with an international socio-ecological-political crisis that inevitably disrupts state-nations, this framework hopes to help consolidate counternarratives empowering pluriversal responsible models of decentralization, and by no means to put down democratic infra-structures simply for the sake of it. At the same time, it refuses to support stagnated models in the hope of taking a step ahead of polarizing discussions, in polyphony and with intellectual responsibility.

According to Vilém Flusser and in the realm of Communicology, intellectual responsibility is the openness to a possible feedback, the openness of a system to another.[38] Responsibility is allowing the receptor to respond, and doing so in such a way that the author is obliged to respond again. Here lies the difference between authority and tyranny. Authority exists when the receptor accepts the author as an emitter; authority is never imposed, but granted by the receptor to the author. Tyranny is when the author imposes itself upon the receptor; therefore, tyranny implies an extreme irresponsibility towards the receptor for not admitting a response. If no feedback is allowed, the receptor becomes "unresponsive" and the author becomes irresponsible towards the receptor. Intellectual authority means the acceptance of an author by its readers, and responsibility occurs when the message is automatically responsive. This is possible by means of ambivalence—the intellectual is responsible when it leaves margins for interpretability, openness to dialogue with other systems.

Responsibility is also a crucial element in Flusser's ontology, which takes place upon the enmeshing of an intersubjective fabric. In his oeuvre, responsibility is synonymous to engagement (in Portuguese, *engajamento*) and evokes a reality that can only be manifested through encounter—the act of realizing oneself through another. We are not subjects acting in relation to objects, we do not find ourselves by navigating an objective world, but we shape our notion of "self" in response to others. Thus, being responsible is the promptness to respond to this confrontation and acknowledge oneself as unrestrained.[39] The responsible is the antagonist of the technocrat, because every engagement results, if successful, not in the realization of a model but in its distortion.[40]

Although Flusser's responsibility concerns mainly critique and the role of sciences, it evokes an embodied dialogue to social, material and environmental circumstances that de-alienates and breaks linearity, allowing access to modes of being manifested through incessant encounter and prompt answerability. With that in mind, and expanding interrelationships among people, objects and places to a broader system of relations among organisms—i.e. ecosystems—it becomes more and more clear that instead of understanding ecology as based on a frame of individual values, an environmentalist approach needs to grow upon relations. In that case, any system of values, language, design, and structure must be as dynamic, as integrated and as processual as the world. Such an approach seeks no salvation and understands no waste—it connects.

The example of *gambiarra* as the mentioning of *favelas*, the parasite and the joker point to the knowledge that can be gained from weaving intersubjective relations to our neighbors—immediate, seemingly careless responses do not exclude responsibility for actions; and in the case of neighbors, it is rather the opposite. Responsibility is a continuous recognition of the impacts and effects of our relation to ourselves, our neighbors and the environment, rather than respect for an assigned norm of conduct, for a rigid social structure reigning over circumstances.

The assumption that we live in an entropic world doomed to overheating and death, to the implosion of its own decay, is the result of an epistemological frame that indeed does not leave room for the new to be manifested. Opposite and concurrently to this paradigm relying on grid-like structures, network behavior tends to continuously increase memory, information and energy; its environmental association systems never cease to exist, they overlay, complement and transform one another.

Curiously, the projects within the formal model of engineer thinking aim to create something new. However, looking at them purely in terms of information, this model only perpetuates itself, allowing very little novelty to emerge, thus its entropic character. Meanwhile, the ecological design model we are trying to elaborate through *gambiarra* departs from existing objects, improvising solutions by means of utilitarian readjustment, and ends up by accumulating and generating something different, extraordinary, and unexpected—i.e. negentropic.

We have seen examples of how lack of governance has led to more oppression, such as neoliberal economic campaigns. Nevertheless, we are still immersed in a hegemonic system fully based on differentiation and subordination. Therefore, the remaining crucial question is how to embrace a non-totalizing approach without succumbing to the prevailing order of things and, in our enthusiasm and lust for life, become ourselves propelling agents for the pasteurization of imagination.

Figure 5. Study of gambiarra networks. Image credits: Monai de Paula Antunes

CONCLUSION

Among uncountable other instances that Wild Design aims to embrace, *gambiarra* is a rare example of design in which human agency does not dominate events but evolves with them. It is rare not because it is infrequent or not present in many places and contexts, on the contrary, it is purposely overlooked as a means to maintain our systems functioning under an hegemonic order—this is how *gambiarra* is relatable to current political, socio-economic, ecological and anthropological discussions and initiatives. Furthermore, evoking *gambiarra* is also a means of going beyond the table of discussion and out there, into the margins, approaching the ecological. The moment is pressing to transcend into other types of human-environment relationships, and *gambiarra* presents an alternative that contributes to building a responsive relation to and with the environment, distancing our initiatives from technological fixes that sustain the dominant modes of living today.

Complexity theory supports an understanding of communication that exposes how collective intelligence evolves in decentralization, displaying the interdependency inherent to ecosystems. In the intersection between ecology and cybernetics, we find many niches in which human agency is manifested in ways other than supremacist. *Gambiarra*, together with *The Parasite* and Flusser's responsibility propose undecidable and indeterminate characters that play an operation liable to enter such a matrix of communication with the environment based on interaction, not good intentions. *Gambiarra* is an example of a contradictory and unfixed practice responsible to the environment in ways that could support environmentalist discourses to move beyond their limitations into more dynamic strategies to deal with the current impasses of human-nature relationships.

The responsiveness inherent in *gambiarra* is a key illustration of the ecological thinking for which this research advocates. Such responsiveness is the equivalent to the abovementioned notion of responsibility that is concerned with overcoming an individualistic human consciousness. Considering design as the human approach to provide for needs and solve problems, Wild Design brings to the center of discussion the need to cut across formal design and engineering that maintain persons in control of processes. And such matrices from human-environment communication are not mutually exclusive: far from eliminating existing structures of knowledge, this framework proposes to question their dominance departing from different principles while avoiding the incorporation of off-grid and plural structures into homogenized systems. That is, it is important to put efforts into harnessing examples of dialogical human agency without pasteurizing them into apparatuses that exclude indeterminacy, contradiction, ambivalence and novelty.

MONAÍ DE PAULA ANTUNES is an artistic researcher, transmission artist and radio-maker interested in complexity and communication together with their material, spatial and political entanglements. She is the director and founder of Archipel Stations Community Radio, and founding and board member of Archipel e.V and Freies Radio Berlin Brandenburg e.V., founding member of Flusser Club e.V. She holds BA, MFA and MA degrees in Visual Communication and Arts and Media, specializing in Generative/Computational Art and Experimental Spatial Systems, all at the Universität der Künste Berlin. She has been awarded the Elsa-Neunmann Fellowship and the Villa Romana Prize. She has exhibited at SAVVY Contemporary, Instituto INHOTIM, Floating University, Onassis Stegi, transmediale, CTM Festival, European Media Art Festival, Ars Electronica and others. She co-edited the Flusseriana: An Intellectual Toolbox—for which she won the prize #6 Deutsche Schönste Bücher 2016 from the Stiftung Buchkunst.

NOTES

1. Rodrigo Boufleur, *A questão da gambiarra: formas alternativas de produzir artefatos e sua relação com o design de produtos* [The gambiarra issue: alternative ways to develop artifacts and its relations to the industrial design] (São Paulo: FAU-USP, 2006), 9 .
2. Rodrigo Boufleur, *Fundamentos da Gambiarra: A improvisação utilitária contemporânea e seu contexto socioeconômico* [The fundaments of gambiarra: the utilitarian contemporary improvisation and its socio-economic context] (São Paulo: FAU-USP, 2013), 3 .
3. Venise Paschoa de Melo & Luciana Martha Silveira, *Coletivo Gambiologia: por uma produção artística em favor do estímulo do pensamento crítico sobre a contemporaneidade* [Gambiology: towards an artistic production in favour of stimulating critical thinking about contemporaneity]. ICONE: Revista Brasileira de História da Arte, 2016, 35. (See also Juliana Gontijo, Distopias Tecnológicas [Technological Dystopias] (Rio de Janeiro: Editora Circuito, 2014).
4. On *gambiarra* and Hacker culture see also Gabriel Menotti, Gambiarra: the prototyping perspective (2010). Conference presentation at the Medialab Prado available online at https://www.medialab-prado.es/sites/default/files/import/ftp_medialab/5/5379/5379_4.pdf. In this presentation, Menotti argues that prototyping and *gambiarra* constitute opposite epistemological and historical perspectives over technological development, yet their state of permanent test phase gains another importance in the present days, when put together with the open source and hackers movement.
5. Fernanda Bruno, "Objetos técnicos sem pudor: gambiarra e tecnicidade" [Unashamedly technical objects: gambiarra and technicity]. *Revista Eco-Pos* vol. 20. 1 (2017): 136. Unless otherwise noted, all translations are the author's.
6. Ibid.
7. For another analogy between gambiarra and Latour's Actor-Network-Theory, see also César Tureta & Bruno Luiz Américo, *Gambiarra as an Emergent Approach in the Entanglement of the Organizational Aesthetic and Technical Controversies:*

The Samba School Parade Case (Brazilian Administration Review Mariga: ANPAD, 2020). By understanding *gambiarra* as creative problem solving based on sensible knowledge applied to deal with controversies, it plays a central role in settling temporary stability for the actor-network of organizing aesthetics. It proposes *gambiarra* to be useful in innovation projects in order to generate creative solutions through prototyping and experimenting, allowing organizations to develop a culture of openness to ambiguity and risk-taking. In their case study, *gambiarra* reveals the entanglements between the hidden world of technicalities and the visible world of aesthetics, that also exposes the entanglements of social and material conditions, being above all, relational.

8. Paulo Faltay Filho, *IMERSom: gambiarras como mestiçagem tecnológica* [IMERSom: gambiarras as technological hybridism] (Florianopolis: ABCiber, 2011).

9. Giuliano Obici, *Gambiarra e experimentalismo Sonoro* (São Paulo: USP, 2014), 10.

10. Ibid.

11. See also Jeimy Lorena Lozano Cadena, *Una Aproximación A Los Laboratorios De Experimentación Desde El Laboratorio De Gambiarras: El Arte De Reutilizar Y Reinterpretar Las Tecnologías* (Bogotá: Universidad Pedagógica Nacional de Colombia, 2018).

12. Wikipedia definition for "Jeitinho" available on https://en.wikipedia.org/wiki/Jeitinho.

13. Maria Fernanda de Mello Lopes, *Gambiarra Como Processo: Uma Antropofagia Latino-americana* (São Paulo: PUC. 2019). Like other authors, de Mello Lopes evokes Brazilian anthropophagism when relating *gambiarra* with technology, "continuing in the desire to devour the foreign, and digest it as something new and their own, working technology as the incorporation of the foreign, modifying it with the appropriation in encounters and fittings to generate new meanings, dynamics, and affective forms of relationship."

14. Helena S. Assunção & Ricardo Fabrino Mendonça, *A estética política da gambiarra cotidiana* [The political aesthetics of everyday kludges] (Rio de Janeiro: Revista compolítica. 2016). The authors present works from Cao Guimaraes and the Gambiologia collective, using Jacques Ranciere's notion of the *distribution of the sensible* to present gambiarra as a creative capacity to reinvent a supposedly established world, leaving unique marks on the collective construction in which we are immersed.

15. Ibid.

16. Janice Perlman, *Favela: Four Decades of Living on the Edge in Rio de Janeiro* (New York: Oxford University Press, 2011), XXIII.

17. *Perlman*, XX.

18. For the length of this article and its focus, the references from Perlman's work, as well as the overall view on the urbanization and internal structures of *favelas,* are constrained to the first 15 years of her research, where organized crime evolving from narcotraffic and the conflicts with the State hadn't yet been established as ruling powers Brazilian *favelas* territories. In Pearlman's words: "When I lived in the favelas in 1968–69, I felt safe and protected, while everyone from elites to taxi drivers to leftists students foolishly perceived these settlements as dangerous. The community was poor, but people mobilized to demand improved urban services,

worked hard, had fun, and had hope. They watched out for each other, and daily life had a calm and convivial rhythm. When I returned in 1999, the physical infrastructure and household amenities were greatly improved. But where there had been hope, now there was fear and uncertainty. People were afraid of getting killed in a crossfire . . . , afraid that their children would not return alive after school, or that a stray bullet would kill their toddlers playing in their verandas. They felt more marginalized than ever." (XXI-XXII). As this paper aims to illustrate *favela* as an open complex network operating through decentralized power,—non-bureaucratic, flexible, spontaneous, non-hierarchic and emancipatory—the complicated implications of narcotraffic and state/milicia violence as authoritarian governments within the *favelas* is too big of a drift from our argument. It is believed that, despite the totalitarianism resulting from organized crime and racial violence in the *favelas*, we can still illustrate through the *favela's* urbanization process and the daily know-how in the dealing with circumstances and neighbors, a complex network behavior that does not follow the protocol of democratic grids. By no means the focus on design, materiality and information theory intends to dehumanize the people and their lives, moreover, this argument stands for a dialogical and transversal deep sense of humanity that is de-alienated, found in the peripheries of predominant human portraits.

19. Ibid.
20. Ibid.
21. Ibid, reference to J.F.C. Turner, "Housing as a Verb," *Freedom to Build* (New York: Macmillan, 1972).
22. Louis Herns Marcelin, "A linguagem da casa entre os negros no Recôncavo Baiano"[The language of house among black people in the Recôncavo Baiano] *Mana. Estudos de Antropologia Social*, 5(2) (1999): 31–60.
23. *Ibid.*
24. Eugênia Motta, "Houses and economy in the favela". Vibrant, 11(1) (1999): 118–158.
25. Ibid.
26. Geísa Mattos, "Favela como quilombo: racialização no enfrentamento da violência do Estado" [Favela as quilombo: racialization in confronting state violence]. Barreira, Irlys; Nilin, Danyelle. (eds.). *A Cidade sob o Chão do Espaço Público*. (Fortaleza: Expressão Gráfica, 2019), 139–158.
27. Mattos refers to the statements and illustrations made by black activists such as Raull Santiago.
28. Mark C. Taylor, *Hiding* (Chicago: University of Chicago Press, 1997), 325–26.
29. Mark C. Taylor, *The Moment of Complexity: Emerging Network Culture* (Chicago: University of Chicago Press, 2001).
30. See John H. Holland, *Hidden Order: How Adaptation Builds Complexity* New York: Addison-Wesley, 1995).
31. Michel Serres, *The Parasite* (Minneapolis: University of Minnesota Press. 1980), 66.
32. Serres, 160.
33. J. Hillis Miller, *Critic as Host, Desconstruction and Criticism* (New York: Continuum Pub Group, 1979).
34. Serres, 36.

35. See Erich.Hörl, *A Thousand Ecologies: The Process of Cyberneticization and General Ecology, The Whole Earth. California and the Disappearance of the Outside*, Eds. Diedrich Diederichsen and Anselm Franke (Berlin: Sternberg Press, 2013),121–130. The article presents several contemporary studies that orbit the intersection between ecology and cybernetics. It cites Gilbert Simondon, Felix Guatarri, Eduardo Viveiros de Castro, Angela Melitopoulos and Maurizio Lazzarato, Jean-Luc Nancy, Katherine Hayles, Jussi Parikka, Mark B. N. Hansen, Luciana Parisi, Timothy Morton, Tim Ingold, Michel Deguy, Bruno Latour, Isabelle Stengers, and Donna Haraway through a whole spectrum of post-humanistic approaches, and many others. Not mentioned in his article and not explicitly evoking cybernetics, we can find similar approaches among scholars of the "New Materialisms," such as Jane Bennett, Pheng Cheah, Melissa A. Orlie and Elizabeth Grosz, who claim that matter matters and contest the subordination of the material world. Karen Barad's work also often supports many critical environmental humanities centered on interconnectedness through her ethico-onto-epistemology based on *intra-activity,* that is, objects do not preceed their interactions and exist in performativity.

36. Beatriz Preciado at the Conference On Seeds and Multispecies Intra-Action: Disowning Life, dOCUMENTA13, during her presentation *Queer bulldogs: Histories of Human-canin Co-breeding and Biopolitical Resistance* on September 10, 2012 in Kassel, Germany.

37. Paraphrasing from Anna Tsing's academic adventures after the network of relations involved in the commerce of Matsutake mushrooms and other complex phenomena that have been neglected by scientific research for lack of appropriate methodology for study. Anna Tsing, *The Mushroom at the End of the World: On the Possibility of Life in Capitalist Ruins* (New Jersey: Princeton University Press, 2015).

38. Vilém Flusser, unknown date. *A Relação entre Ciência e Praxis: A responsabilidade do cientista* [The Relation Between Science and Praxis: The Responsibility of the Scientist]. Audio content from the Vilém Flusser Archive Berlin.

39. Steffi Winkler, "Responsability," in *Flusseriana: An Intellectual Tool Box* (Minneapolis: University of Minnesota Press,2016), 342–3.

40. Vilém Flusser, unknown date. *Do Desengajamento.* Unpublished manuscript, Vilém Flusser Archive.

Towards a Newer Analytical Frame for Theorizing Ethnic Enclaves in Urban Residential Spaces

A Critical Dialectic Approach in Relational-Spatiality

NAWAL SHAHARYAR

Abstract

This paper provides a critical reflection on the nature of ethnic enclaves and segregation by presenting an analytical frame that can be used to capture the contested nature of spatiality in these spaces. By underscoring the dynamics in which differences constitute distinct subject positions, this paper posits a relational orientation to studying spatiality that is based on complex relations among and between subjects and space. To date, few attempts have been made to present an analytical frame for the analysis of the spatiality of ethnic enclaves and segregation in which space becomes contested by different groups, occupants of space, and those external to space. This paper bridges this gap by synthesizing the relational approaches found in Bourdieusian field theory and Lefebvrian spatiality.

This paper seeks to make three contributions. First, to provide an explicit theoretical anchor upon which relational and spatial theories converge since the underlying rationale for complementary is usually only implicitly evaluated. In detailing this convergence, the social constitution of reality and an emphasis on the duality between individuals and society as well as society and space are identified as a rationale for relational spatiality. Second, to demonstrate how a collective engagement with Bourdieu's and Lefebvre's approaches facilitates a recognition of spatiality as a polysemous social product and producer of social reality in addition to grounding this orientation as a critical dialectic engagement in which both the subjects and knowledge production cannot be neutral. Third, to present an analytical frame for the investigation of ethnic enclaves in and through which ethnic majorities, minorities, occupants of space, and those external to these enclaves constitute different views towards the same space.

INTRODUCTION

Recent years have been marked by an increase in relational and spatial theories of the city and urban complexity.[1] These theories contain numerous differences, and this diversity of spatial metaphors can be seen as theoretical tools that work in conjunction with the relational turn.[2] Together, they broaden the theoretical space for the study of complex and socio-spatially embedded phenomena of cities, that recognize the intimate connections between the "structural" and the "discursive."[3]

However, the relational-spatial context of ethnic enclaves and their associated spatial segregation in urban residential spaces remain relatively undertheorized, particularly of residential spaces largely occupied by ethnic minorities. These include "ghettos," "slums," "downtowns," and densely populated urban districts such as African-American spaces that discursively become known as the "hood" in American contexts. These spaces are typically spaces in which ethnic minorities exist as the majority occupants.[4] However, there have been few attempts to present these spaces from the vantage point of both majorities and minorities in the same space. Specifically, research on how and why the same space has different meanings for different ethnic groups, occupants of space, and those external to space remains underdeveloped. In this context, a relational-spatial synthesis is needed to better understand the contexts in which one space can contain, produce, and reflect multiple modes of being and belonging- as well as perspectives, demands, memories, and associations that stem from varied social and spatial relations.[5]

This paper outlines a means for bridging this gap by drawing on the relational approach found in Bourdieu's field theory and Lefebvrian engagement with cities, particularly Lefebvrian insights on the production of space.[6] This synthesis provides the three main contributions of this paper. Firstly, it provides an explicit theoretical anchor upon which relational and spatial theories converge. This has the additional advantage of anchoring Bourdieusian field theory and Lefebvrian spatiality as particular readings since numerous interpretations of both can be found in the literature.[7] Secondly, it seeks to advance a critical dialectic approach within relational spatiality that treats space as a complex phenomenon drawing in different subject positions that are internal and external to space. Thirdly, it presents an analytical frame for critical

engagement in the investigation of contested positions in spatiality between dominant and dominated groups, occupiers of space, and those
external to it.

This paper is divided into three sections. The first section explores
avenues of convergence for the relational-spatial approach in contrast
to earlier substantive approaches. The second section examines recent
scholarship in relational-spatiality to demonstrate how a deeper engagement with Bourdieu and Lefebvre widens the analytical arena for
the investigation of difference in space. The second section thus argues
how a synthesis of Bourdieu and Lefebvre paves the way for a critical dialectic approach to studying ethnic enclaves and segregation in urban
residential spaces. The third section presents an analytical frame for
investigating differences in subject positions in a relational vocabulary
of dominant and dominated positions inside and external to space.
Thus, the third section focuses on production and produced space
from numerous, overlapping, conflicting, and possibly contradictory
subject positions. For instance, in the example of African-American
neighborhoods above, this insight can be used to analytically explore
African-American residents and white residents in a neighborhood
and in relation to the wider social contexts of both populations outside
the residential arena under investigation. This orientation calls into
question the analytical significance of scales in theorizing differences
in space.[8] For example, what is this wider African American or white
context, and is it limited to the city or the state? Or does it draw in a
much larger theoretical orientation towards race politics in the United
States of America, which has a history of slavery, contemporary social
movements, such as Black Lives Matter, and more? This orientation to
spatiality is arguably more dynamic, context specific, and relational. It
includes complex relationships that collectively shape urban space, in
contrast to theories of urban space that cater to only minority or majority ethnic groups, and subject positions.

TRACING THE OVERLAPS BETWEEN RELATIONAL-SPATIAL THEORIES

This section presents the theoretical backdrop against which relational and spatial theories converge in the rejection of; substantive

theories, ontological dualism, and value neutral knowledge production. In underscoring convergence, Bourdieusian and Lefebvrian insights can be used to examine the differences among and between subjects in spatiality.[9]

Beyond Substantive Theories—Emphasizing the Constitution and Context of Social Reality

Emily Erikson argues that relationalism is a contested term.[10] Through an examination of the magna opera of relational texts,[11] she argues that the breadth of relationalism can be understood as "a theoretical perspective based in pragmatism that eschews Cartesian dualism, substantialism, and essentialism while embracing emergence, experience, practice, and creativity."[12] Thus, relationalism is an anti-essentialist orientation that accounts for the formative and dynamic role of processes in social phenomena. In the manifesto for relational sociology, a cornerstone of relational philosophy,[13] Mustafa Emirbayer argues that relationalism rejects the essentialism hitherto found in social theories, which perceive society as static, reified categories of structures and agents. He argues that methodological individualism and ontological structuralism hold the same substantialist perception of social reality as "self-sustaining entities which are 'preformed' and only then . . . consider the dynamic flows in which they subsequently involve themselves."[14] In contrast, the relational view demonstrates how interaction itself shapes the constitution of social phenomena. However, Emirbayer argues that relational thought is underscored by a transactional orientation in which entities can only emerge, exist, and embed themselves in dynamic relationships within a particular context. Thus, context is of primary significance since nothing exists outside of the dynamic processes that constitute a particular relationship. From Marx to Foucault, Emirbayer traces the complex sets of relationships that reveal how capital and power are not concepts in themselves but are complex social configurations and arrangements. He argues, "Far from being an attribute or property of actors, . . . they emerge out of the very way in which figurations of relationships—as we shall see, of a cultural, social structural, and social psychological nature—are patterned and operate."[15]

This insight is two-fold, in that relationships are the ontological primary in social contexts and are also the social agents and structures being constituted. This separates the relational turn from previous theoretical orientations. Empirically, the relational turn has often been interpreted through the lens of either a deep processualism or a relational-structural approach,[16] with the former emphasizing dynamic processes as the locus of emergence and the latter combining "static, structural orientations" and dynamic processes in the constitution of social phenomena. Despite these differences, emphasis is placed on relational emergence and constitution of social phenomena in both.

Theories of spatiality are even more heterogeneous, which has led to differing opinions among scholars.[17] Generally though, emphasis is placed on how researchers should move away from considering space as a stationary background towards perceiving space as a constitutive element of society.[18] Kirsten Simonsen argues that theories of spatiality do not simply see space as one element of constitution in a wider set of social relations. Instead, these theories contend that spatiality both produces different constitutions, and is produced by these constitutions of beings, bodies, and discourses in space.[19]

In short, while relational theories invert the analytical relation between substance and processes by prioritizing processes in the constitution of phenomena, theories of spatiality shift emphasis to the constitution of space as a lived social dimension and product. This departure from substantive theories is the first aspect of complementarity.

Dualism versus Duality

Both relational and spatial theories seek to discard the theoretical binaries that produce antinomies of agents and structures. Luk Van Langenhove differentiates between dualism and duality by stating that the former views agency and structure as mutually exclusive aspects, while the latter treats them as two sides of the same coin.[20] Namely, duality states that agent and structure can be understood as the medium and outcome of social action. In the case of relationalism, antinomies are a reification of social processes into "reductive entities."[21] Instead, it is important to determine the agent and structure as emergent properties in specific relationships that are both meaningful and constitutive.[22] Hence, emphasis is placed on duality in which specific relationships co-exist and constitute social phenomena.

Spatial theories have also emphasized the need to overcome dualism that populated earlier traditions. David Harvey contends that the theories of space have evolved from an absolute conception of space towards a relative and, recently, relational orientation.[23] The absolute conception of space was the dominant model for a long time, mirroring the ethos of Newtonian space in which the natural world was seen as a rigid impartial homogenous space for objects, entities, and observers.[24] In this view, space was treated as a continuous backdrop upon which elements of the social were played out. The assumption that the physical, natural, and material world were real and stood outside of the social, symbolic, and mental worlds led to a dualism between physically inert spaces and socially active spaces.[25] As a point of departure, the relativist and relational view embed themselves in Einstein's and Leibniz's conceptions of space, in which space cannot exist independent of the bodies and positions in it. However, subtle differences between the two conceptions remain as the relativist view prioritizes action-centric approaches often adhering to classic dualism, while the relational view abandons dualism for an emphasis on the constitutive aspects of social relations. It is within the relative and relational conception that space has moved away from emphasizing objects towards emphasizing subjects, intentionality, processes, and constitutive dynamics.[26]

However, few scholars explicitly engage in conceptualizing how spatiality overcomes dualism. Eden Kinkaid argues that the dualism between agent and structure obscures how politics, space, agency, and structure act as mediums and outcomes in creating differences among and between bodies.[27] Therefore, a central claim in theories of spatiality is arguably an emphasis on the duality of the individual in society rather than a dualism separating the two.[28] A further instance of duality in spatial theories is also evident in the duality between the social and the spatial. Just as individuals are constituted in and through society, so too is space constituted in and by the social. A more explicit engagement that captures this duality of space can be seen in Edward Soja's orientation to space.[29] In forwarding a socio-spatial dialectic,[30] Soja argues that spatiality rests on three interrelated principles:

1. A constitutive role of space in shaping agents, structures, beings, individuals, and communities;
2. Spatiality as a social medium and outcome in which space is social, dynamic, and changeable; and
3. A web of relationships in and through which space shapes the social and the social shapes the spatial.

Thus, spatiality is a constitutive element of the social in which the traditional binaries between the individual and the spatial and the social and the spatial are replaced by a duality of the individual in society and the socio-spatial. In this context, the insistence on duality follows from the insistence that spatiality is both produced and producer of difference.[31] This shared orientation towards duality of social phenomena is the second aspect of convergence.

Rejecting Value Neutral Theory

Epistemic claims on the impossibility of objective value-neutral socio-scientific knowledge are also shared by both theories. In exploring the relations between researcher, research, and positionality, relational theories contend that knowledge production occurs in a wider web of historical and scientific relations.[32] Spatial theories have rejected the possibility of value neutrality for both historical and theoretical reasons through which spaces have been envisioned as complex social phenomena embedded in historical, cultural, regional, and social values.[33] The insistence that spatiality is produced in context and from viewpoints eliminate the possibility of analyzing space objectively. Rather, the analysis of space requires explicit engagement with positionality, the context of socio-culturally produced space and knowledge relations.[34] Therefore, the third aspect of convergence between these theories resides in the socio-spatially embedded context of knowledge.[35]

This theoretical complementarity between relationalism and spatiality in the examination of constitutive claims, the insistence on analytical structuralism through the rejection of ontological dualism, and the rejection of value neutral epistemological engagement collectively pave the way towards the relational-spatial approach.

Towards Relational Spatiality

Recently, theorization of the urban has drawn from the relational-spatial approach without acknowledging the approach holistically. From Engin Isin's accounts of the constitutive role of the city in citizenship to Ash Amin's exploration of ethnic diversity in urban settings, various connections between relationalism and spatiality have been posited.[36] Furthermore, literature on the urban in complex entanglements of the relational and spatial as well as between nature, the environment, material reality, and symbolic constraints has also gained prominence in the last two decades.[37] However, in the literature, relational spatiality as a theoretical approach remains partial, fragmentary, and selective.[38]

The most notable scholarship that explicitly defines itself within the relational-spatial approach is Martina Löw's work, which is insightful in demonstrating the theoretical orientation of relational spatiality and its current limits.[39] She synthesizes the materiality of objects and bodies to the structural, symbolic, and experiential dimensions of the social world. Löw contends that spatiality is a relational arrangement of living things and goods stemming from two interlinked processes of "spacing" and "synthesis." She contends that spacing is understood in terms of placement of people and social goods that are primarily symbolic, while synthesis is seen as the linking of goods and people via perception, imagination, and memory. It is through synthesis that goods and people come to represent duality between materials and symbols. Her approach presents a unique way forward in synthesizing the structural and symbolic as well as the relational and the spatial, and it provides insights into how subjects come to be constituted in spatiality.[40] Through an overview and synthesis of earlier works in human geography, Löw explicitly underscores how subjects and space are co-constituted within a duality in which neither can be seen as independent of the other.

However, her approach leaves little room for explicit engagement with the concept of spatial difference and its constitutive effect on inequalities.[41] Although Löw recognizes that the structure of spatiality produces and maintains social inequalities of class and gender, she does not explain the emergence of diverse and often unequal subjects within one spatiality. It has been argued that her orientation obscures how spacing occurs in a relational triad between goods and people within a space and how it extends to others outside the space.[42] Thus, the social constitution of space is not only limited to the socio-demographic characteristics of the occupants of space, but it involves those external to a specific spatial arrangement. In short, an approach to spatiality has to be created that recognizes the means by which different subjects shape the constitution and meaning of space both internally and externally. Drawing on this insight, this paper demonstrates how relational spatiality can be used to theorize difference in positions and orientations within contested, complex, and conflicting constitutions of space. The next section demonstrates how Bourdieu and Lefebvre collectively pave a way for this relational-spatial examination of ethnic enclaves and segregation in urban contexts.

BOURDIEUSIAN FIELDS AND LEFEBVRIAN PRODUCTION OF SPACE—DIALECTICS OF SPACE AND FIELDS

Bourdieu posits that the social world should be conceptualized in the fields of production, circulation, and consumption. The constitution of fields is intimately tied to forms of power that are connected to the dialectic interplay between a person's position in the field and habitus.[43] Bourdieu's treatment of fields rests on a two-fold dialectic: one between capital, habitus, and field and the other on the structuring and structured effects of the field.[44] This two-fold dialect acts as the locus of constitution for manifold positions in the field.[45] It is here that subject positions are differentiated from each other, and it is within this differentiation that asymmetrical relations of power manifest themselves. By underscoring power asymmetries in the constitution of the field and subject positions, the subjects lose essentialist features as pre-given entities and become relational elements that are constituted in webs of contestation, struggle, differentiation, and (mis)recognition.[46]

In spatiality, Doreen Massey argues that "differences" are the social relations of space that are experienced and interpreted differently by different subject positions.[47] This leads to the recognition that difference always implies a difference in space in which non-dominant subjects are constructed as distinct from dominant subjects.[48]

Explicating Bourdieusian fields has two distinct advantages. First, it allows for the exploration of how the same space can constitute different subject positions articulated in distinctions that represents asymmetric power relations leading to hierarchies among people.⁴⁹ Second, it leads to the recognition of the ways in which differences in subject positions within the field are not only related to a localized space as they refer to all fields in and across space that overlap to create hierarchies, asymmetries, and differences. In this context, relational spatiality in terms of the constitution of subjects in space needs to account for the wider dynamics in and beyond a space. In the study of ethnic enclaves and segregation of urban spaces, such a focus allows for the identification, mapping, and explanation of the manifold subject positions of dominated and dominant groups in various positions to each other and to space. Thus, differentiation and differences in constitution are not just between dominant and dominated groups as they involve residents within a district and those external to the urban space under investigation.⁵⁰ Essentially, explicit engagement with Bourdieusian field theory allows for the examination of the relations within a space and the relations external to space, and it facilitates the recognition of the differences in subject positions as open, dynamic, and contested positions in the field.

In coupling Bourdieusian field analysis with Lefebvrian production of space, the explicit means by which spaces in urban centers come to be constituted for different ethno-spatial positions can be made explicit. Thus, the constitution and articulation of differences rest on three interlinked dialectics: the constitution of subject positions in power asymmetries between dominant and dominated positions, the structuring and structured effects of fields, and the dialectics of subject positions and geographies.

Reading the Production of Space in Bourdieusian Fields

In seeing space as a produced reality, Lefebvre draws heavily from Marxist dialects but moves beyond static conceptions by incorporating fluid social processes.⁵¹ Lefebvre argues that space is a politically contested field as spatiality rests on three elements coming together: representations of space (conceived space), representational space (perceived space), and spatial practice (lived space)⁵².

For Lefebvre, representations of space have physical manifestations from material aspects, such as infrastructure and built environments, to symbolic displays that categorize, sort, or frame spaces, such as maps and other referential materials. However, representational space radiates the prominent and often conflicting symbolism that shapes space. Representational space is therefore best understood as a discursive sphere that is embedded in representations of space and spatial practices. Furthermore, spatial practices are spaces that are coded by active human interaction that embodies the daily practices and actions of the users of a space. These interactions frame experiences within a space and, in doing so, affirm the ideals, symbols, and asymmetries in space.[53] Here, spatiality and its effects are constituted by both contestation and struggle within each element of the spatial triad and among components of the spatial triad.[54] In this context, empirical investigations have often explored the tensions between representations of space and spatial practices in urban contexts.[55] However, the context in which these differences are constitutive of different subject positions remains underspecified.

By advocating for a merger between Bourdieu and Lefebvre, the constitution of different positions can be studied in the context of asymmetries of the field. In short, the explicit synthesis calls attention to the means by which different subject positions in and about space are produced, and it creates possibilities for analyzing the context in which these positions relate to wider systems. Thus, Lefebvrian spatiality presents a Bourdieusian field in both theoretical and empirical terms that delineate the field in the form of concrete spaces, such as neighborhoods, towns, villages, and cities, while drawing in elements external to the space under investigation. This synthesis facilitates a recognition of differences in space for positions in the field.

The centrality of dialectics in the production of space, differences, subject positions, and fields indicates how this approach is best understood ontologically as a dialectic relational-spatial approach. Furthermore, by explicating Bourdieusian fields as analytical constructs that are separate from social reality, a critical epistemology can be presented.

EPISTEMOLOGICAL INSIGHTS—FIELD AS CONSTRUCTS

The shared rejection of value neutral knowledge presents a particular epistemic orientation in which knowledge is selective, partial, and fragmented. Bourdieu utilizes relational insights to bridge the dualism between objective and subjective thought. He posits that "the point of view is a perspective, a partial subjective vision (subjectivist moment); but it is at the same time a view, a perspective, taken from a point, from a determinate position in an objective social space (objectivist moment)."[56] This epistemology draws in manifold social positions in order to determine social constructions of reality, and it calls for a dialectic engagement between theory and empirical verification, thereby enabling a plurality of constructs that reflect social reality to emerge.[57] Field analysis thus calls for a critical awareness of the epistemic implications of representing social reality from subjective orientations within an objective "moment."[58] Field analysis opens up the analytical space to determine various positions allowing a plurality in theoretical investigations. This epistemology facilitates critical and genealogical investigations of analytical fields.[59]

Similarly, the epistemological consideration of space centralizes the significance of spatial constitution and its structuring effect on social reality.[60] In the ontological recognition that subject positions are constituted, located, and contested in space, a universal representation of spatiality removed from subjects and their positions in society becomes impossible. Judith Gerber demonstrates how the social production of a natural order is itself a reification of socio-spatial dynamics.[61] Indeed, even in demarcations of territory and statehood, Lefebvre demonstrates the political and cultural characteristics of materiality, architecture, boundaries, cities, and nations.[62]

A synthesis of Bourdieu and Lefebvre on these ontological and epistemological grounds can be seen as a critical dialectic approach within relational spatiality. The next section presents an analytical space in which this approach can be used to study spatiality of urban spaces dominated by minority subject positions.

ENVISIONING ETHNIC ENCLAVES AND SEGREGATION THROUGH SPATIALITY AND FIELDS

The discussion above has paved the way for a critical dialectic approach to the study of ethnic marginalization in the city in three distinct terms. Firstly, by recognizing that city spaces are differently constituted for different subject positions, a larger orientation to social, cultural, and ethnic enclaves and segregation can be achieved.[63] Secondly, by underscoring the significance of dialectics in the formation and maintenance of asymmetrical fields and subject positions, an explicit dialect relational-spatial approach can be determined. This approach opens up relational analysis among and between different subject positions from majority and minority subject positions within and outside space. Thirdly, the recognition that socio-spatial fields (material, social, symbolic, and discursive aspects) converge in society reveals the means by which power is exercised in shaping marginalized spaces. Furthermore, it also creates avenues for response in terms of resistance, transformation, and adaption. By acknowledging that social perception is connected to different elements of the spatial triad, from conceived space (the purview of governments and agencies) to spatial practices (where residents themselves engage in social and symbolic actions in daily life), the critical dialectic approach can be applied to any aspect of the socio-spatial dialect either on its own or in relation to other elements of the spatial triad. The realms of possibility opened up by this approach enable researchers to explore diverse social positions in a particular social space.[64] This allows for a deeper understanding of the dynamics that frame spaces without the reification of any one subject position. Furthermore, this facilitates a recognition that fields as analytical constructs emanate from specific spaces in which constant, active, and critical engagement is required to capture the field as a contested social reality.

Towards an Analytical Frame for Studying Ethnic Enclaves and Segregation via Spatiality and Fields

The collective engagement with these three aspects results in the production of a general analytical model. Although there are numerous ways in which to construct this analytical field in relation to the space under investigation, the table below demonstrates how ethnic minorities and their residential spaces can be studied within a dialectic orientation in relational-spatiality.

Contested Spatiality of Residential Space or Neighborhoods

SPATIAL TRIAD	OUTSIDE SPACE		INSIDE SPACE	
	MAJORITY SUBJECT POSITION	MINORITY SUBJECT POSITION	MAJORITY SUBJECT POSITION	MINORITY SUBJECT POSITION
Conceived Space	Policy makers and city planners		Capacities for participation: Official, formal, and informal politics	
Perceived Space	Symbols and ideas circulating in society about neighborhoods and their connection to other spaces		Contestation between generalized social symbols and local representations, meaning making, and "frames"	
Lived Space	Extent of engagement and forms of interaction with residents of a space		Embodied experiences, memory, livelihood, and belonging	

Although, this table presents a binary between outside and inside spaces it retains the relational context in which the ethnic majority interacts with the minority in and across space. Additionally, this analytical representation allows for the exploration of the contested and competing orientations that are differentiated not only along ethnic and social lines but also across spatial lines when determining how residential spaces come to be produced as different and contested spatialities.

Each row and column of the table can be studied individually and comparatively. For instance, the majority or minority subject position towards any one aspect of the triad (conceived, perceived, or lived space) can be determined. The differences in subject positions reflect the varied positions of the majority and the minority, which are inside and outside spaces. This orientation allows one to account for conceived spaces from the vantage point of policy makers and urban developers,[65] and extends the analysis to participatory frameworks in policy for different subject positions.[66] Similarly, in the investigation of perceived space, the diversity of symbolism that constructs the space from various subject positions can be investigated. This facilitates the study of complex contestations of symbols from different perspectives towards the space.[67] For instance, Eugene J McCann examines the means by which the public spaces in American cities reflect racialized features represented by contradictory discourses in which black public spaces are seen as "unsafe hoods" for the wider population and as "black cultural spaces" for the inhabitants of these spaces.[68] Moreover, the diversity of embodied experiences within and outside spaces can also be investigated to reflect varied or similar experiences in the same space.[69]

Furthermore, in the table, each subject position can be investigated by examining the dynamic interplay between two or more aspects of the spatial triad, such as the majority subject position outside space based on an investigation of conceived and perceived space and the majority subject position based on an investigation of conceived and lived space, amongst others. In addition, each subject position can also be studied in the production of spatiality based on the four interconnected aspects of the spatial triad (majority subject position outside space, majority subject position inside space, minority subject position outside space, and the minority subject position inside space). This analytical field facilitates the investigation of the dialectic relations in which the majority and minority subject position come to be constituted in any one aspect of the spatial triad, such as how the majority and minority subject positions relate and differ in terms of conceived space, perceived space, and lived space. Lastly, this analytical frame has the unique advantage of being able to investigate spatiality as a whole in relation to other subject positions and orientations to space.[70]

The explicit recognition that both dominant and dominated subject positions emerge in relational fields of asymmetric power relations underscores the dynamics by which majorities and minorities come to be constituted. This highlights the dialectic relation by which spatiality is produced and maintained. The engagement with Bourdieusian fields and the Lefebvrian production of space thus paves the way for analyzing the complex webs of relations that exist in producing and maintaining different constitutive relations towards residential spaces that are largely occupied by minorities from the perspectives of minorities and majorities within and external to space across conceived, perceived and lived space.

CONCLUSION

This paper has contributed to the growing literature on the relational and spatial turn on three grounds. First it has presented a theoretical anchor upon which relational spatiality can be understood in contrast to substantive approaches. In this context, a newer relational vocabulary of asymmetric differences in fields and subject positions has been put forward to overcome substantive static theorizations of ethnic enclaves and segregation in residential spaces.[71] Second the centrality of dialectics has been emphasized. It has been argued that spatiality should be seen as a dialectic relationship between the social and spatial that emerges from the interplay between conceived, perceived, and lived space. Furthermore, it has been argued that Bourdieusian fields should be ontologically understood as a two-fold dialectic: for the emergence of different subject positions in the context of an asymmetrical field and between the structuring and structured effects of the field. By locating the dialectics of constitution in relational webs, the importance of studying spatiality in wider social entanglements has been emphasized. Similarly, two-fold dialectics have been emphasized epistemologically, as a dialectic between objective and subjective positions within the field and a dialectic between analytical and real fields. Drawing on these elements, this paper's third contribution is the presentation of an analytical frame that can be used to investigate the contested nature of urban residential spaces that are largely occupied by dominated subject groups. This analytical frame seeks to investigate spatiality from different subject positions of ethnic majorities and minorities as well occupants of the space and those external to space. In presenting this analytical framework, the paper invites critical dialogue and reflection in studying space beyond isolated investigations of conceived, perceived, or lived spaces.[72]

Taken together, a critical dialectic orientation has been presented that can be used to collate diverse literature within the relational-spatial approach to create an avenue for investigating differences in space. This holistic approach aims to bridge gaps that exist in the critical analysis of the contested and manifold constructions of spatiality for different subject positions in a relational vocabulary of dominated, dominant positions, insiders and outsiders in space.

NAWAL SHAHARYAR is a lecturer and early career researcher, pursuing her doctoral studies at the school of Law, governance and Society at Tallinn University, Estonia. Her research examines the social construction of spaces and is focused on the socio-political implications of ethno-linguistic segregation in urban residential spaces of Tallinn, Estonia.

NOTES

1. For discussions on the contemporary relevance of cities in globalization, emancipation, and more, see Ash Amin, "The good city," *Urban Studies* 43, no. 5–6 (2006): 1009–1023; Ash Amin and Stephen Graham, "The ordinary city," *Transactions of the Institute of British Geographers* 22, no. 4 (1997): 411–429. For a detailed discussion on spatial planning and complexity, see Patsy Healey, *Urban complexity and spatial strategies: Towards a relational planning for our times* (London: Routledge, 2006).
2. Ilana Friedrich Silber "Space, fields, boundaries: The rise of spatial metaphors in contemporary sociological theory," *Social Research* (1995): 323–355.
3. For a discussion on how the material, structural, and psychological can be seen within scientific and methodological relationism that combines substantive and relational orientations under one theoretical umbrella, see George Ritzer and Pamela Gindoff, "Methodological relationism: Lessons for and from social psychology," *Social Psychology Quarterly* (1992): 128–140; Mauro Dorato, "Is structural space time realism relationism in disguise? The supererogatory nature of the substantivalism/relationism debate," *Philosophy and Foundations of Physics* 4 (2008): 17–37.
4. Various aspects of ethnic enclaves that lead to segregation and inequality have been well-researched in terms of capital flight from downtowns to suburbs as well as downtown revitalization. See Bernard J. Frieden and Lynne B. Sagalyn, *Downtown, Inc.: How America Rebuilds Cities* (Cambridge. MA: MIT press, 1991); Meagan M Ehlenz, Deirdre Pfeiffer, and Genevieve Pearthree, "Downtown revitalization in the era of millennials: How developer perceptions of millennial market demands are shaping urban landscapes," *Urban Geography* 41, no. 1 (2020): 79–102.
5. However, recently theorization on the contested nature of space in relation to ethnic, industrial, de-industrial, and global cities has seen renewed rigor. For a good introductory overview of how urban sites connect broad socio-cultural phenomena to individual experiences and produce different orientations and contestations, see Setha M. Low, "The anthropology of cities: Imagining and theorizing the city," *Annual Review of Anthropology* (1996): 383–409.
6. For Bourdieu, see Pierre Bourdieu, *Distinction: A Social Critique of the Judgement of Taste* (Cambridge, MA: Harvard University Press, 1984); Pierre Bourdieu, "What makes a social class? On the theoretical and practical existence of groups," *Berkeley Journal of Sociology* 32 (1987): 1–17; Pierre Bourdieu, *The Logic of Practice* (Stanford University Press, 1990); Pierre Bourdieu, *Practical Reason: On the Theory of Action* (Palo Alto, CA: Stanford University Press, 1998); Pierre Bourdieu,

Jean-Claude Chamboredon, and Jean-Claude Passeron, "The craft of sociology," in *The Craft of Sociology* (De Gruyter, 2011). For Lefebvre, see Henri Lefebvre, The Production of Space, D. Nicholson-Smith, Trans., (MA: Blackwell 1991); Henri Lefebvre, "The right to the city, 'Eleonore Kofman and Elizabeth Lebas, Trans., in *Writings on Cities* (Oxford: Blackwell Oxford, 1996); Henri Lefebvre, *Key Writings* (London: Bloomsbury Publishing, 2017); Henri Lefebvre, Sacha Rabinovitch, and Philip Wander, *Everyday Life in the Modern World* (London: Routledge, 2017).

7. For instance, Bourdieu has been interpreted as a structural constructivist. See Loïc JD Wacquant and Pierre Bourdieu, *An Invitation to Reflexive Sociology* (Cambridge: Polity, 1992). He has also sometimes been seen as a relational phenomenologist. See Will Atkinson *Bourdieu and After: A Guide to Relational Phenomenology* (London: Routledge, 2019). However, Lefebvre has been seen as theorist within critical phenomenology. See Eden Kinkaid "Re-encountering Lefebvre: Toward a critical phenomenology of social space," *Environment and Planning D: Society and Space* 38, no. 1 (2020): 167–186. For recent relational spatiality research, see Joseph Pierce and Deborah G. Martin, "Placing Lefebvre," *Antipode* 47, no. 5 (2015): 1279–1299.

8. The discussion on the ontological significance of various scales in relational thought are beyond the scope of this paper. However, a good overview of the idea in which scales relate to broader meanings, politics, space, and temporality can be found in Danny MacKinnon, "Reconstructing scale: Towards a new scalar politics," *Progress in Human Geography* 35, no. 1 (2011): 21–36.

9. Consider the insights from post-structural theory on the constitution of differences between people. Rey Chow summarizes this by demonstrating how difference precedes identity since meaning itself requires active anchoring to generate sense. Furthermore, Bernard E. Harcourt demonstrates how the moment in which meaning is imposed, ascribed, attributed, or discerned is not based on a singular orientation but emanates from fluid and multiple interpretations. This insight inverts the link between difference and identity, and it places emphasis on how difference creates an identity or an object of study. Rey Chow, "The interruption of referentiality: Poststructuralism and the conundrum of critical multiculturalism," *The South Atlantic Quarterly* 101, no. 1 (2002): 171–186; Bernard E. Harcourt, "An answer to the question: 'What is poststructuralism?' University of Chicago, *Public Law Working Paper* 156 (2007). For a detailed discussion on how difference relates to ethnic identity in post-structural theory, see Rajagopalan Radhakrishnan, "Ethnic identity and post-structuralist difference," *Cultural Critique* 6 (1987): 199–220.

10. Emily Erikson, "Relationalism emergent," *Contemporary Sociology: A Journal of Reviews* 44, no.1 (2015): 3–7.

11. Two influential books on the theory and practice of relational research are Christopher Powell and François Dépelteau (Eds.), *Conceptualizing Relational Sociology: Ontological and Theoretical Issues* (New York: Springer, 2013); François Dépelteau and Christopher Powell (Eds.), *Applying Relational Sociology: Relations, Networks, and Society* (New York: Springer, 2013)

12. Erikson, "Relationalism Emergent," 03.

13. Mustafa Emirbayer, "Manifesto for a relational sociology," *American Journal of Sociology* 103, no. 2 (1997): 281–317.
14. Emirbayer, 1997: 283.
15. Emirbayer, 1997: 292.
16. For a discussion on the difference between these approaches, see Frédéric Vandenberghe, "The relation as magical operator: Overcoming the divide between relational and processual sociology," in *The Palgrave Handbook of Relational Sociology*, François Dépelteau (Ed.) (London: Palgrave Macmillan, 2018): 35–57.
17. For a detailed overview of key differences within theories of spatiality, see Phill Hubbard and Rob Kitchin (Eds.), *Key Thinkers on Space and Place* (New York: Sage, 2010).
18. This can be seen across a diverse range of literature on human geography and the constitution of space.
19. Kirsten Simonsen maps different theoretical orientations to space into three main categories. In the first category, an emphasis is placed on the built environments (from David Harvey's analysis of constructed space as fixed capital to Foucault's analysis of materiality disciplining society found in the ideas of panoptic). In the second category, space is conceived as a difference in material and symbolic aspects and contributes to social processes. In the third category, space is considered a fundamental aspect of constitution, from localized daily practices to the large-scale global organization of labor, wealth, power, and the like. It is in this third category that spatiality is a produced reality and also an arena in which difference is constituted and played out. A detailed overview can be found in Kirsten Simonsen, "What kind of space in what kind of social theory?" *Progress in Human Geography* 20, no. 4 (1996): 494–512.
20. Luk Van Langenhove, "Varieties of moral orders," *Frontiers in Sociology* 2, no. 9 (2017): 1–13.
21. Nick Crossley, *Towards Relational Sociology* (Routledge, 2010).
22. Mustafa Emirbayer and Ann Mische, "What is agency?" *American Journal of Sociology* 103, no. 4 (1998): 962–1023.
23. David Harvey, *Social Justice and the City*. Vol. 1. (Athens, GA: University of Georgia Press, 2010).
24. It is crucial to note that, within the absolute conception, there was no singular approach to space but different modes of envisioning space as a fixed container or background category.
25. For a discussion on the binaries (actual, virtual, extensive, and intensive) of space and its relation to post-structural theoretical orientations, see Manuel DeLanda, "Space: Extensive and intensive, actual and virtual," *Deleuze and Space* (2005): 80–88.
26. For a brief overview of Newtonian versus Euclidean space and its implications in human geography, see Stuart Elden, "Space I," *International Encyclopedia of Human Geography* 10 (2009): 262–267.
27. Eden Kinkaid, "Re-encountering Lefebvre: Toward a critical phenomenology of social space," *Environment and Planning D: Society and Space* 38, no. 1 (2020): 167–186.

28. Nicky Gregson, "On duality and dualism: The case of structuration and time geography," *Progress in Human Geography* 10, no. 2 (1986): 184–205.

29. Edward W Soja and Costis Hadjimichalis, "Between geographical materialism and spatial fetishism," *Antipode* 11, no. 3 (1979): 3–11; Edward W Soja, "The socio-spatial dialectic," *Annals of the Association of American Geographers* 70, no. 2 (1980): 207–225; Edward W. Soja, *Postmodern geographies: The Reassertion of Space in Critical Social Theory* (London: Verso, 1989); Edward. W. Soja, "Writing the city spatially," *City* 7, no. 3 (2003): 269–280.

30. Soja, "The Socio-Spatial Dialectic," 1980.

31. See note 19.

32. For a detailed discussion the epistemic foundations of relationalism, see Osmo Kivinen and Tero Piiroinen, "Toward pragmatist methodological relationalism: From philosophizing sociology to sociologizing philosophy," *Philosophy of the Social Sciences* 36, no. 3 (2006): 303–329.

33. For one of the earliest works on the specificity of urban spatiality and its relations to macro structures and individualized experiences, see Kurt H. Wolf (Ed.), *The Sociology of Georg Simmel*. Vol. 10 (New York: Macmillan Publishers, 1950). Moreover, an emphasis on critical theories in the context of cities and the transformative capacities of the city can be seen across scholarship of space. For a detailed historical overview, see Phil Hubbard and Rob Kitchin, *Key Thinkers on Space and Place.*

34. For a typology of major relational frameworks (practice theory, pragmatism, network analysis, and positional and process-oriented analysis) and their orientation towards normative knowledge production, see Patrick Thaddeus Jackson and Daniel H. Nexon, "Reclaiming the social: Relationalism in Anglophone international studies," *Cambridge Review of International Affairs* 32, no. 5 (2019): 582–600.

35. Steven Shapin, "Placing the view from nowhere: Historical and sociological problems in the location of science," *Transactions of the Institute of British Geographers* 23, no. 1 (1998): 5–12.

36. For a few examples in which relational spatiality is implicitly invoked, see Engin Fahri Isin, *Being Political: Genealogies of Citizenship* (Minniapolis, MN: University of Minnesota Press, 2002); Engin Fahri Isin, Ed., *Recasting the Social in Citizenship* (Toronto: University of Toronto Press, 2008); Engin Fahri Isin, "Citizenship in flux: The figure of the activist citizen," *Subjectivity* 29, no. 1 (2009): 367–388; Ash Amin, "Ethnicity and the multicultural city: Living with diversity," *Environment and Planning A* 34, no. 6 (2002): 959–980; Ash Amin and Nigel Thrift, "Cities and ethnicities," *Ethnicities* 2, no. 3 (2002): 291–300. This list is not exhaustive but is indicative of the means by which different relational orientations are tied to constitutive understandings of spatiality.

37. See, for instance, Lisa Benton-Short and John Rennie Short, *Cities and Nature* (London: Routledge, 2013); Gert De Roo and Jean Hillier, *Complexity and Planning: Systems, Assemblages and Simulations* (London: Routledge, 2016).

38. For a detailed critique, see Peter Sunley, "Relational economic geography: A partial understanding or a new paradigm?" *Economic Geography* 84, no. 1 (2008): 1–26;

Martin G. Fuller and Martina Löw, "Introduction: An invitation to spatial sociology," *Current Sociology* 65, no. 4 (2017): 469–491.

39. To trace relational spatiality as an explicit theoretical framework, see Martina Löw, "The constitution of space: The structuration of spaces through the simultaneity of effect and perception," *European Journal of Social Theory* 11, no. 1 (2008): 25–49; Martina Löw, "The intrinsic logic of cities: Towards a new theory on urbanism," *Urban Research & Practice* 5, no. 3 (2012): 303–315; Martina Löw, *The Sociology of Space: Materiality, Social Structures, and Action* (New York: Springer, 2016); Hubert Knoblauch and Martina Löw, "On the spatial re-figuration of the social world," *Sociologica* 11, no. 2 (2017): 1–27.

40. Löw, "The sociology of space . . .", 2016.

41. For a discussion on the significance of theorizing socio-cultural, socio-symbolic, or economic differences, see Katherine McKittrick and Linda Peake, "What difference does difference make to geography?" *Questioning Geography: Fundamental Debates* (2005): 39–54.

42. For a critique of how Martina Löw's orientation cannot account for difference in and among subjects and a short reply, see Martina Löw and Gunter Weidenhaus, "Borders that relate: Conceptualizing boundaries in relational space," *Current Sociology* 65, no. 4 (2017): 553–570.

43. Rachel Fensham, Terry Threadgold, Jen Webb, Tony Schirato, and Geoff Danaher, *Understanding Bourdieu* (London: Routledge, 2020).

44. This paper is inspired by the interpretation of Lizardo's work on Bourdieu. For a detailed explanation of the relationship between field and habitus in structuring the field, see Omar Lizardo, "The cognitive origins of Bourdieu's habitus," *Journal for the Theory of Social Behaviour* 34, no. 4 (2004): 375–401.

45. This insight on the locus of constitution for manifold positions in the field in relation to capital, habitus, and field itself is explicitly discussed in Peter Jackson, "Chapter 9: Pierre Bourdieu" in *Critical Theorists and International Relations*, Jenny Edkins and Nick Vaughan-Williams (Eds.) (London: Routledge, 2009).

46. The relational orientation of the subject implicated in webs of constitution, contestation, recognition and misrecognition is outlined in Pierre Bourdieu & Nice, *Outline of a Theory of Practice* (Cambridge: Cambridge University Press 1977); Pierre Bourdieu, *Logic of practice* (Translated by Richard Nice), (Palo Alto, CA: Stanford University Press 1990).

47. Doreen Massey, "Concepts of space and power in theory and in political practice," *Documents d'Anàlisi Geogràfica* 55 (2009): 15–26.

48. For an in-depth discussion of space and constitutive role in subject positions of difference, see McKittrick and Peake, "What difference . . ." 2005.

49. Bourdieu himself develops this argument in great detail in his work *Distinction*. See note 6.

50. For empirical investigations using these relational ideas of different subject positions and their manifold relations in ethnic enclaves as well as segregation and inter-ethnic dynamics, see Andreas Wimmer, "The making and unmaking of ethnic boundaries: A multilevel process theory," *American Journal of Sociology* 113, no. 4 (2008): 970–1022; Jaeeun Kim, "Ethnic capital, migration, and citizenship: A Bourdieusian perspective," *Ethnic and Racial Studies* 42, no. 3 (2019): 357–385;

Raivo Vetik, "National identity as interethnic (de)mobilization: A relational approach," *Ethnopolitics* 18, no. 4 (2019): 406–422.

51. In theorizing how Lefebvre relates to Marxist dialectics and spatial theory, this article draws heavily on the ideas presented in Mark Gottdiener, "A Marx for our time: Henri Lefebvre and the production of space," *Sociological Theory* 11, no. 1 (1993): 129–134; Eric Sheppard, "Geographic Dialectics?" *Environment and Planning A* 40, no. 11 (2008): 2603–2612.

52. The idea that space can be treated as a field that is political and contested is articulated in Stuart Elden, "There is a politics of space because space is political: Henri Lefebvre and the production of space," *Radical Philosophy Review* 10, no. 2 (2007): 101–116; Lefebvre, *Production*, 33–34 and 38–46.

53. Jenny Bauer, "Thirdings, Representations, Reflections," in *Perspectives on Henri Lefebvre: Theory, Practices and (Re)Readings*, Jenny Bauer and Robert Fischer (Eds.) (Berlin: De Gruyter Oldenbourg, 2019): 207–224.

54. For a discussion on a constitution that is born through dynamic interactions within each element of the triad and among elements, see Michael Leary-Owhin, "A fresh look at Lefebvre's spatial triad and differential space: A central place in planning theory?" In *2nd Planning Theory Conference University of the West of England*, 2015: 1–8.

55. Note that, in empirical exemplification, emphasis is placed on politically contested dynamics, representations, and discourses in the production of space in order to underscore the means by which different orientations to a space emerge. See Husik Ghulyan, "Lefebvre's production of space in the context of Turkey: A comprehensive literature survey," *SAGE Open* 9, no. 3 (2019): https://doi.org/10.1177 /2158244019870537.

56. Bourdieu, "What makes a social. . . .", 1987: 2.

57. Karl Maton, "Reflexivity, relationism, & research: Pierre Bourdieu and the epistemic conditions of social scientific knowledge," *Space and Culture* 6, no. 1 (2003): 52–65.

58. For a detailed discussion on how antinomies and dualism between objectivity and subjectivity can be overcome in the works of Bourdieu, see Omar Lizardo, "Beyond the antinomies of structure: Levi-Strauss, Giddens, Bourdieu, and Sewell," *Theory and Society* 39, no. 6 (2010): 651–688.

59. For instance, this epistemic orientation problematizes the links between realism, rationalism, and relationalism. Such epistemic insight calls into question the notion of objective reality from subjective prior positions. For a detailed discussion on how this epistemic insight goes to the roots of social science theory, see Timothy Rutzou, "Re-imagining social science," *Journal of Critical Realism* 15, no. 4 (2016): 327–341.

60. By incorporating spatiality in investigations of space, one can move beyond both geographical materialism and spatial fetishization in which a reified primacy of space is advocated. For in-depth engagement with this epistemic foundation beyond the reification of space, see Edward W. Soja and Costis Hadjimichalis, "Between geographical materialism and spatial fetishism," *Antipode* 11, no. 3 (1979): 3–11.

61. Judith Gerber, "Beyond dualism—The social construction of nature and the natural and social construction of human beings," *Progress in Human Geography* 21, no. 1 (1997): 1–17.

62. Henri Lefebvre, "Space and the State," in *State/Space: A Reader,* Neil Brenner, Bob Jessop, Martin Jones, Gordon Macleod (Eds.), (Boston: Wiley-Blackwell, 2008): 84–100.

63. For empirical exemplifications that implicitly rely on these theoretical foundations, see Kafui A. Attoh, "What kind of right is the right to the city?" *Progress in Human Geography* 35, no. 5 (2011): 669–685; Doreen Massey, *Space, Place and Gender* (Cambridge: Polity Press, 2013).

64. Mike Raco, "Living with diversity: Local social imaginaries and the politics of intersectionality in a super-diverse city," *Political Geography* 62 (2018): 149–159.

65. For an empirical case that implicitly holds this theoretical orientation towards conceived space, see Mark Purcell, "Excavating Lefebvre: The right to the city and its urban politics of the inhabitant," *GeoJournal* 58, no. 2 (2002): 99–108.

66. For a discussion on participatory urban policy and design, see Alexandre Apsan Frediani and Camillo Boano, "Processes for just products: The capability space of participatory design," in *The Capability Approach, Technology and Design,* Ilse Oosterlaken and Jeroen Van den Hoven (Eds.) (New York: Springer, 2012): 203–222.

67. For a theoretical engagement on how Lefebvre effects the symbolic and semiotic studies of space, see Pentti Määttänen, "Semiotics of space: Peirce and Lefebvre," *Semiotica* 166 (2007): 453–461. For an empirical instance, see Andrzej Zieleniec, "The right to write the city: Lefebvre and graffiti," *Environnement Urbain* 10 (2016): https://doi.org/10.7202/1040597ar.

68. Eugene J McCann, "Race, protest, and public space: Contextualizing Lefebvre in the US city," *Antipode* 31, no. 2 (1999): 163–184.

69. See, for instance, Melanie Dodd, (Ed.) *Spatial Practices: Modes of Action and Engagement with the City* (London: Routledge, 2019); Chris Butler, *Henri Lefebvre: Spatial Politics, Everyday Life and the Right to the City* (London: Routledge-Cavendish, 2012).

70. An implicit utilization of this approach is seen in Ng et al.'s investigation of Hong Kong's Piers saga. By exploring the constitution of spatiality of the Star Ferry and Queen's Pier, the authors demonstrate how different subject positions from pre-World War II colonial orientations to modern state perspectives shape the dynamics in which spatiality is constructed for average citizens. In this context, the spatiality of the majority subject position outside space can be seen in relation to the majority subject position in space, minority subject position in space, and minority subject position outside space. See Mee Kam Ng, Wing Shing Tang, Joanna Lee, and Darwin Leung, "Spatial practice, conceived space and lived space: Hong Kong's 'Piers saga' through the Lefebvrian lens," *Planning Perspectives* 25, no. 4 (2010): 411–431.

71. For a detailed discussion on the need for a newer relational vocabulary to theorize cities, agency, and citizenship, see Engin Isin, "Citizenship in flux: The figure of the activist citizen", *Subjectivity* 29, 367–388 (2009).

72. See, for instance, the contexts in which these studies move beyond focusing on only one element of the spatial triad: Michael Buser, "The production of space in metropolitan regions: A Lefebvrian analysis of governance and spatial change," *Planning Theory* 11, no. 3 (2012): 279–298; Sam Halvorsen, "Spatial dialectics and the geography of social movements: The case of Occupy London," *Transactions of the Institute of British Geographers* 42, no. 3 (2017): 445–457.

Book Reviews

Cartographic Memory: Social Movement Activism and the Production of Space
BY JUAN HERRERA
Durham, N.C.: Duke University Press, 2022

REVIEWED BY AÍDA R. GUHLINCOZZI

Juan Herrera's historical recounting of Latino activism in Fruitvale, California, in *Cartographic Memory: Social Movement Activism and the Production of Space* is stellar. In fact, the case focused on by Herrera as an example of activism producing space and creating change in the name of social justice is not the only top-quality contribution to Latinx geographies to be found in this book. Herrera's conceptualization of "cartographic memory" builds on the intertwining of Latinx writers and historians with traditional spatial thought from the history of geography. His definition of "cartographic memory" as a "political remaking of urban geography and therefore a selective mapping" adds to the broader oeuvre of activism and space coming out in recent years (14).

The geographic location for *Cartographic Memory* comes from the author's long history of working in and around Fruitvale as both a volunteer and community member. As a new resident of the Oakland area, Herrera mistakenly navigated himself to Fruitvale, where he found the elements of the place clearly speaking to a cultural aesthetic of Latinidad. Intrigued, Herrera began volunteering in the area, and learned more of the long activist history of the space. That activist history, Herrera argues, has long been under-studied, or even forgotten, in Chicano activist history, and merits recognition. Herrera's efforts with this book go a long way to gathering together that spatial history and reconstructing it for the reader through interviews and oral histories with numerous activists, extensive archival research, and ethnography focusing on the 1960s and 1970s Mexican-American activist mobilization in support of the Chicano movement.

The power of the focus on Fruitvale must be recognized, as Herrera also makes space for intently peeling apart the layers of nonprofit funding, social movements, and community-building and support. The chapter, "Revolution Interrupted," is about the funding situation of the Unity Council in Fruitvale and how the funding structure was constructed over time in the context of the political and economic opportunities of the 1960s. It speaks to how this had a profound effect on the organizers and community given the shift from grassroots to institutional funding. This chapter opens the book with a focus on the national scope of funding opportunities for organizations in the 1960s that focused on race and ethnicity. Through this lens are explored the effects of local political actions—such as the 1969 speech by San Antonio-based Mexican American Youth Organization (MAYO) leader Jose Angel Gutierrez—on funding at the federal level. Because of the perceived militancy of these remarks, the U.S. Congress became concerned, and eventually passed the 1969 Tax Reform bill, limiting the types of projects that could be funded philanthropically. This type of multi-scale understanding of Fruitvale activism is threaded throughout the entire book, from chapter 1, "Making Place," in which Herrera summarizes activist perspectives on Fruitvale as emphasizing "not only how the neighborhood *itself* [produced] a geography of activism but also how it was interconnected to other places of struggle throughout the United States" (emphasis in original; 33).

Herrera also navigates the interactions of race, ethnicity, and space, tracing how coalitions, influences on political efforts, and collaboration took place throughout Fruitvale and Oakland during this period. His second chapter, "The Other Minority," identifies where Black Panther Party-related work occurred; the marketization that began to occur of a non-threatening, non-Black "Latino" identity; the effect that this had on activist efforts; and more. Importantly, in this chapter Herrera's interviews reveal that part of the interest in these coalitions came from the clear organizational success Black activists had achieved in their work, leading Mexican American activists in Oakland to pursue similar efforts. One interviewee, Herman Gallegos, a prominent activist at the time, spoke of recalling an event where Black men would gather monthly to focus on leadership. Thinking highly of them, he says that he recognized them as future "mayors, judges . . . [but] kept thinking: Where are we? We are not anywhere! We are not visible!" (76). In advocating for community needs, Gallegos and other Mexican American activists are described as reaching out to and collaborating with Black organizers to develop alliances and push for civil rights. One interviewee, Alex Zermeño, is described as stating "Our only power was to join with the Black community, and their agenda was the same as ours. You know, civil rights, civil rights, civil rights!" (77).

Herrera's contemplations on race, space, place, and activism in his book on cartographic memory and Fruitvale are full of heart, rich historical references, interviews, and imagery. A key contribution is Herrera's call for scholars examining social movements to include in their analyses the "openness of space" (174), as social movements often produce institutions and spaces that live on beyond the "end" of the social movement. Drawing from Doreen Massey's understanding of space as a set of "loose ends and missing links," Herrera identifies the Fruitvale history of Chicano movement activism as a site for social space that is continuing to develop. With this effort, Herrera argues that time and space work in concert to enable social movement activism to continue to create ripples that shape the "neighborhood politics, resources, and conditions of possibility for activism today" (174).

Herrera also importantly is informed by the critical work of Katherine McKittrick, Laura Pulido, Lisa Cacho, and other scholars of race and geography in his understanding of social movement activism and spatial production. Herrera recognizes how racial capitalism, colonialism, and the intertwining of race and geopolitics help shape the experiences of activists in Fruitvale and the conditions of their activism. With this book, Herrera displays the activism of the Chicano movement, exploring it for new threads of conversation on the issues of race and space. Instead of taking the common approach of trying to center the Latino activists of the movement, Herrera weaves their experiences into the larger milieu of Fruitvale, Oakland, and the U.S. overall, from funding to racial dynamics in activism. This approach enables Herrera to confront the recent critiques of Latinidad, activism, and race and ethnicity narratives within the Latine community. By displaying a case of coalitional work from the beginning, with activists attributing much of their inspiration and first steps to being supported by the Black activist movement, Herrera puts forth a new, more inclusive and nuanced story that he identifies as only a "story-so-far." This book will helpfully inform the next generation of geographers, activists, and students on the crucial impact space has on social movements, and the ways social movements shape space and place.

The Porch: Meditations on the Edge of Nature
BY CHARLIE HAILEY
Chicago: The University of Chicago Press, 2021

REVIEWED BY BRUCE B. JANZ

Charlie Hailey's *The Porch* is a difficult book to review. This is not because I have to be measured in my praise—it is an excellent book, well written, with a mix of close observations and rigorous research. It is also not difficult to review because it is challenging to read—it is an absolute joy to read. Hailey is a writer with a sense of rhythm and scene; this work could easily be taught in a course on creative nonfiction as it has that sense of writing craft along with its phenomenological acuity.

No, *The Porch* is difficult to review because I get the sense that Hailey is asking us to do something other than evaluate it for the adequacy of its arguments or the originality of its points, or even the beauty of its writing. He is asking us to enter a world with him, to see things we haven't seen and see those we have seen in a new way. The chapters are titled "Porch," "Tilt," "Air," "Screen," "Blue," and "Acclimate," and these give an idea of the space he is opening up. It is a space somewhere between a material world and the sense we make of it. The author is entirely committed to both, but not fooled by the illusions or uplifting promises of either.

The primary porch of the book is on his cabin on the Homosassa River in Florida. It is a porch that is under threat of rising waters due to climate change and catastrophe due to hurricanes. It is a porch on an estuary fed by a spring, which means that the water quality and clarity varies greatly over the nine miles of the river's flow. Animal life abounds. It is, in other words, a porch where one is not going to be easily lulled to sleep, at least if paying the slightest bit of attention.

It is perhaps unavoidable that talking about this book means talking about the environment. Indeed, on a first reading, this reminded me more of nature writing than architecture writing. The book is, to be sure, a reflection on architecture at its best, which is to say, the lived aspect of built space, the almost imperceptible but nonetheless real ways in which the liminal space of the porch affords the experience of the membrane between nature and culture, the outside and the inside, the public and the private. But it is also nature writing, inasmuch as a common thread in nature writing is to place us in the middle of nature, as part of it. We are not the designers, nor are we the inhabitants; we are those in the milieu, the middle of cause and effect, actor and acted upon, subject and object. It is a rare book on architecture, even vernacular architecture, that achieves this. The tendency is to always look for the optimization of the built environment, the tweak that will succeed in drawing us out into our best selves or the cute or trendy new feature. That is not Hailey's goal here.

If the porch is one of the best places in the built environment to understand the milieu, it must present itself in those terms beyond the author's own circumstance. Otherwise, this would just be a paeon to a much-loved place. But the book is full of examples of porches, both literary and real, not just as objects or as liminal spaces between nature and culture, but as sites that show us their inhabitants and guests in unguarded and exploratory moments. If the trope of human vs. nature in American letters is of the human coming to terms with his or her own individuality, striving to tame, dominate, or at least fit into nature, and the trope of human in the built environment often ends up as the externalization of our internal, as-yet unrealized natures, this porch does something entirely different. We neither have the self/other relationship, nor do we have the external/internal dynamic. And, in Hailey's hands, the porch is not just a transition space either, something that facilitates moving through to one of the more "real" spaces of the interior or exterior. The phenomenology is different. He brings the porch into reality, the reality we've always known it had but that is virtual, fleeting, easy to overlook. Hailey's porch is not just on the way to a place—it is a place.

But it is not a place of power, either. It is not just the place from which announcements and speeches are made, although it can sometimes be that too. It is not just the place of observation of the life that goes by on the street or the town or in nature, the space of interpretation. Hailey does not deny these functions, but he focuses elsewhere.

As is often the case, the end of the book organizes and makes sense of the rest of the book. Hailey's last chapter is "Acclimate." This term comes up earlier, when he outlines St. Gregory of Thaumaturgus's stages of penance, which involve entry into the church through the outer porch of the narthex. It is the process of return to the source, and as he puts it at the end of the account, "For those who had fallen away from the church, this system of penance was a process of re-acclimation" (114).

"Acclimate" has echoes of Watsuji Tetsuro's idea of Fu-do, translated as "climate" in the title of his book *Climate and Culture*. It is climate, yes, but some translate Fu-do as "milieu"—that which we are in the middle of. Watsuji takes a broadly revisionist Heideggerian look at how place matters to forms of life; Hailey's scope is much more fine-grained. The porch is the space where we most deliberately open the interior to the exterior and vice versa. It is the place where we can be most aware of the milieu. Hailey sets the book up to explore all the ways in which we can be aware of our milieu. These ways involve the construction of the porch itself, its dimensions and "tilt" (the title of the second chapter), but also its functions of preserving memory, encountering the new, and in some sense challenging one's own settled habits.

Hailey has two chapters—"Air" and "Screen"—that, in a sense, stand in contrast with each other. Air flows through, a continuous agent, whereas screen separates, allowing flow but not unlimited flow (ideally, blocking things such as insects). Being in the milieu means engaging the new, whereas having a screen means that the new is not just randomness but has some minimal structure and separation. A screen is a filter. Hailey goes into some detail describing the history of the weave of the screen, the optimal dimensions that filter in just the right way. Porches are not patios open to the world, but are circumscribed in the back, away from casual passers, even if they afford similar kinds of leisurely human activity. They are not courtyards, wholly surrounded by structures or standing as oases in the midst of activity. Porches often need the demarcation of a screen, or at least the symbolic line of an edge. The screen, though, is a recognition of the life that happens or that one might hope happens on the porch.

So, the tension between air and screen is a kind of milieu because we never leave life or retreat from it or take a timeout. There is always encounter, or at least the potentiality of encounter. This is what Hailey captures throughout this book in his close observation of the construction of the porch and in the various accounts of porch life as seen through Southern writers such as Marjorie Kinnan Rawlings, Zora Neale Hurston, Harper Lee, and Flannery O'Connor; musicians such as the Allman Brothers, Beyonce, and Crosby, Stills, and Nash; and philosophers such as Maurice Merleau-Ponty and John Dewey; and many others.

This is not, in other words, just an introspective look at *his* porch, but a truly phenomenological exercise in teasing out the experience of the porch and the experiences that the porch affords. The tension between air and screen is an example of this. In showing both continuity and rupture, we have an inter-face—a place where the vitality of a place is something other than an unreflective habituation of that place, but it can be raised to reflection without being destroyed by the act of reflecting. We sometimes think of the primary virtue of interfaces in the digital world as seamlessness and invisibility, but in fact the best interfaces inter-face—that is, allow recognizability and legibility across difference. There are haptics to feed back information, design differences on physical interfaces to promote differentiation, and so forth. We recognize and value the seamlessness, but that is only made possible by the differentiation made in well-designed interfaces.

Hailey's porch is an inter-face of this sort. It is not a control panel that an operator might use to effect change, but is rather a place where the screen and the air operate together to provide the kind of life in the world that promotes exploration and connection to others through history who have sat on their own porches and understood themselves anew by doing so.

Most of Hailey's chapters have a sense of this meeting of the world and the self. His fifth chapter, "Blue," comes closer to introspection:

"But we have to practice seeing *in, through,* and *around* what we're looking at. And a porch, immersed in the blue of its imagination, helps us do that" (205). Blueness feels contingent—a color he chose to paint the ceiling of the porch—but he sees past that contingency to the symbolic nature of blueness as the perceived color of sky and water. It is another meeting place of inside and outside, this time not in the tension between the flow of air and the interface of screen, but in the symbolic references of blueness.

We know that it is symbolic blueness that is at stake here, because a major example used in the chapter is that of the Resurrection Chapel at the Woodland Cemetery in Stockholm, Sweden, designed by the architect Sigurd Lewerentz in 1920. Hailey traveled there to experience all the porches in the cemetery, including the one to the Monument Hall. Even in pictures it is vast and imposing. Unlike Hailey's own porch ceiling, these are not blue, but that's not the point here. The porch to the Resurrection Chapel—in its openness to the world and its transitional function to inner, solemn space—serves to bring the blueness into the inner world, at least a little. Hailey fortuitously (in retrospect) forgot to bring his tape measure, and so his architect's eye was forced towards recognizing the human scale, along with the "imperfections" that were too large to be mistakes (especially by such a major architect), and that made the porch something other than a colonnade meant to communicate grandeur and precision over the world. He paced out the space instead of measuring, using his boots to identify small deviations from what many architects might have done, and in using his body he experienced the porch: "Its blue is a splinter I still trace" (184).

By the end of the book, Hailey has moved us fully into nature. We are with John Muir in his "hang-nest," his suspended cabin in Yosemite. It's a sort of porch, at least it's a space for viewing what's going on. "For Muir, the hang-nest cradled a love of nature" (234). It is another version of the milieu: "In another letter to his sister, Muir wrote: 'I do not live "near the Yosemite," but in it—in the very grandest, *warmest* center of it'" (emphasis in original; 237). This has been Hailey's goal all along—not just to look at the porch as a liminal space, as the edge between nature and the built environment, but as that which, almost more than any other space, puts us in the middle and keeps us there.

Like Hailey, I live in Florida. I don't have a porch, though—no one on my street does. My house was built in the 1980s, well after the advent of air conditioning, and the thinking was that technology would make this place livable by controlling inhabited places, thus undermining the need for the porch. What has functioned as a milieu space for me has been walking on the Cross Seminole Trail every morning, for years at this point (until recently, I had been out every day for over three years). It has afforded a social aspect to the neighborhood, a way of resisting the isolation that air conditioners produce. If the porch is a pre-air conditioner liminality in Florida suburbs, something else seems to be required to even approach some of the elements of the porch as Hailey describes it. There is an effort needed when there's no porch. It is possible to acclimate to the trail, like a porch, meeting people and being in the middle of life, but it's no porch. But as I continue to walk, I take the rich reflections of Hailey's book with me, and look for those precarious, hopeful glimpses.

The Nature of Space
BY MILTON SANTOS (TRANS. BY BRENDA BALETTI)
Durham, N.C.: Duke University Press, 2021

REVIEWED BY DAVE McLAUGHLIN

When asked to review Milton Santos's *The Nature of Space,* I was interested mostly in the book's core theme. As a literary geographer, my own research focuses heavily on space as an analytical concept and a lived experience; I was keen to read and understand a fresh perspective on this topic. Little did I know that opening this book would connect me to a world of geography scholarship for the most part ignored, actively or otherwise, in the Anglophone academy. For my sins, I was not alone in this ignorance. In 2017, for example, one scholar felt confident in writing that:

> The English-speaking geographical community knows very little about
> the theoretical work in geography being produced in the so-called

"global South." They are unaware, for example, of the work of Brazil-ian geographer Milton Santos.[1]

It is not my place here to write about the reasons why this is such a mistake. Others, better qualified than me, have already done so.[2] My aim here is to do three things. First, to put Santos's arrival into English-language geography in context; second, to consider briefly his key contribution to defining the nature of space; and finally, to touch on what Santos's book offers us more broadly.

Published in 2021, Brenda Baletti's translation of Santos's great work arrived on the crest of a wave of discussions, debates, and scholarly interventions around decoloniality in Western geography. This movement emphasizes uncovering "still colonising frames of knowledge"[3]—frames "through which the world is apprehended and explained and modelled for the future"—and "craft[ing] ways of thinking harder about and against them."[4] Others have argued that the long wait for an English translation of Santos's *The Nature of Space* is evidence of just such modes of thought continuing, unreflectively, among Anglophone academia. In 2019, an English-language translation of Santos's *For a New Geography* was published by the University of Minnesota Press, followed by *The Nature of Space* in 2021. Hopefully, publications indicate that some publishers, at least, are following Stephen Legg's call to think hard against certain predominant Western frames.

The Nature of Space, despite its mere 280 pages, is an opus of sorts. Santos's style eschews narrow conceptualization in favor of building a solid theory of space on a remarkably broad foundation of thinkers, including Braudel, Merleau-Ponty, Habermas, Latour, and many, many others. This broad foundation is a result not only of his long career and his own widely travelled life; it is necessary due to the slippery and almost-undefinable nature of space itself. In a wonderful section of *For a New Geography,* Santos lays out the problem facing geographers in defining this concept around which our discipline revolves:

> I understand why geographers have spent more time defining geogra-phy than space as the latter is extremely hard to do. The same could be said of space as Saint Augustine said of time: "if I ask myself if I know

what it is, I respond that I do; but, if I ask myself to define it, I respond that I do not know how."[5]

Part of this complication, recognized by Santos, is that "space" is a word with many meanings outside academia.[6] Yet, geographers also face no simple task in defining this core concept for our own needs. Doreen Massey's definition from *For Space* is one of my favorites, not only because it well illustrates the complexity of the term "space," but also due to the range of reactions it produces in my first-year undergraduate students when I introduce it: Space is the sphere of the possibility of the existence of multiplicity in the sense of contemporaneous plurality.[7] This is a very crunchy sentence! But it gets to the heart of a conceptually complex truth: that space is the dimension in which things *happen,* a dimension in which we must live at all times, as well as seek to better analyze and understand.

Santos's solution to this problem is, as far as I am concerned, a masterstroke. Rather than seeking analytical terms outside of the world, his analytical construction co-opts terms and understandings from within life and combines them in theoretically-informed ways to build a theory of space that is analytically complex but at once lived in the world. His top-line definition of space is as "indissoluble systems of objects and systems of actions" (5). Yet, the indissoluble nature of space *in fact* does not mean that we, as scholars, cannot analyze it at lower levels of operation. An important part of Santos's conception of space is that it contains within it internal analytic categories, including landscape, territorial organization, the territorial division of labor, produced or productive space, roughness, and content-form (5).

As with other theorists of space, such as LeFebvre, here space is both whole and yet composed of different types, or kinds, or processes of space. These compositional "things" are objects or processes from within the world, such as landscape, but are also "spatial areas . . . [and] region, place, networks, scales . . . [and] the environment." They serve a dual purpose, as both "internal analytic categories," which relate back to a totalizing conception of lived space, and as things-in-themselves. In this way, Santos's theory reads as both intellectually consistent and cognizant of the breakages and connections between theory (of the world) and practice (in the world).

Beyond its complex yet enlightening theory of space, Santos's work impacts on geography scholarship and our lives in the world in other important ways. As Baletti writes of the act of translating *The Nature of Space,* contemporary digital technology and its decontextualization and globalization of society are a central concern for Santos, despite his book being written a quarter-century before our current time of social media and ever-present smartphones. As Baletti argues, Santos's aim in revealing this undercurrent shaping our lives is to encourage us to look not outside of it, because that would be virtually impossible (no pun intended), but rather within and through it, and so to work to embed localizations and real connections in this new world.[8] This is a salutary lesson for geographers, for whom, as James Ash et al. argued so recently, "the turn to the digital in geography has, to a large degree, been thoroughly internalized and *taken for granted.*"[9]

NOTES

1. Lucas Melgaco, "Thinking Outside the Bubble of the Global North: Introducing Milton Santos and 'The Active Role of Geography,'" *Antipode* 49, no. 4 (2017): 946.
2. Jörn Seemann and John C. Finn, eds., "JLAG Book Review Forum: The Nature of Space," *Journal of Latin American Geography* 21, no. 2 (2022): 192–221.
3. Stephen Legg, "Decolonialism," *Transactions of the Institute of British Geographers* 42, no. 3 (2017): 347.
4. Sarah Radcliffe, "Decolonising Geographical Knowledges," *Transactions of the Institute of British Geographers* 42, no. 3 (2017): 329; Legg, "Decolonialism," 347.
5. Milton Santos, *For a New Geography* (Minneapolis: University of Minnesota Press, 2019), 89.
6. Ibid.
7. Doreen Massey, *For Space* (London: Sage), 31.
8. Brenda Baletti, "The Nature of Space by Milton Santos (review)," *Journal of Latin American Geography* 21, no. 2 (2022): 219.
9. James Ash, Rob Kitchin, and Agnieszka Leszczynski, "Digital Turn, Digital Geographies?" *Progress in Human Geography* 42, no. 1 (2018): 26; emphasis added.

Spatializing Culture: The Ethnography of Space and Place
BY SETHA LOW
London: Routledge, 2017

REVIEWED BY CARLOS J. L. BALSAS

Spatializing Culture: The Ethnography of Space and Place adds clarity to our understanding of the value of ethnographic scholarship in the study of socio-economic, cultural, and developmental transformations. The book is a thorough review of two established conceptual frames of analysis—the social production of space and the social construction of space—coupled with an in-depth discussion of four newer ways to make sense of the world around us: embodied space, language and discourse, emotion and affect, and translocal space. As the world is transformed by a myriad of forces and events occurring simultaneously, its complexity intensifies insurmountably and we require clear and robust concepts, theories, methods, and tools to not only interpret it, but above all to attempt to change it in ways that are more beneficial to our collective co-existence while enabling the flourishing of those most at risk.

Readers of *Spatializing Culture* will find plentiful theoretical constructs, lineages, diverse viewpoints, examples, and overall opportunities for reflecting on how the (built) environment, spaces, and places have been changing mostly due to our behavior. Inspired by Foucault's take on genealogy, in chapter 2, Setha Low traces the history of space and place according to distinct interpretative schools of thought ranging from philosophical and mathematical, French social theory, geographical, architectural, environmental psychology, to anthropological, and even archeological. Five Venn diagrams are utilized to illustrate the main conceptual relationships between space and place. Most of the book's in-depth case studies were researched by the author with only a small number investigated and written up by fellow scholars, which Low utilizes in the book with gratitude. The interrelated thematic and distinct geographical scope of the cases is one of the book's hallmarks. The illustrative case studies come from such faraway places as Latin America (San José, Costa Rica), Asia (Taipei, Taiwan), North America (New York City; Washington, D.C.; Philadelphia, Pennsylvania; and San

Antonio, Texas), Southern Europe (Smederevska Palanka, Serbia), and the Middle East (Beirut, Lebanon; Cairo, Egypt; and Tel Aviv, Israel).

Spatializing Culture was first mentioned to me years ago by a former colleague at the University at Albany, SUNY. His ongoing work in Latin America, coupled with his ethnographic training and prior work in a region of the world also extensively examined by Low in other scholarly works, was likely the reason for bringing it up in a conversation about the latest developments in the field and potential research opportunities. I acquired the book when I was teaching Global Urbanism and Culture and International Urban Planning. I was pleasantly surprised with the book's thorough conceptual lineage, historic characterizations, attention to detail, comprehensive ethnographic investigations, and implications for transforming reality as well as institutional processes. *Spatializing Culture* is a welcome addition to urban planning textbooks, which tend to be relatively less critical, are often covered with normative constructs and statistics, and are more institutional in their characterization of problems and recommendations for further action.

For the most part, the ethnographic method is qualitative, participatory, detailed, and quite comprehensive in characterizing key variables as the researcher found them on the ground. This differs slightly from urban planning's preoccupation with public policy, policy analysis, rules and regulations, institutionalized procedures, the public good, and overall positivist and rationalist concerns with documenting reality and helping to lead transformative planning processes, whether in the realm of land use, transportation, housing, economic development, infrastructure, or the environment. Although International Urban Planning was to be taught in a rather orthodox manner with recourse to understanding planning cultures, best practices, lessons learned, and implications for similar situations, the Global Urbanism and Culture course was slightly more aligned with the discussions put forward by Low. These included attention to postmodern ideals, the use of creativity in community planning, distinctions between popular and highbrow culture, and the building of iconic structures in contexts of urban regeneration and mega-event planning. As such, my students were somewhat already exposed to issues of embodied spaces and to ideas of how places are not only constructed and codified by regulations and discourses but also perceived—if not experienced—by owners, renters, residents, tourists, and visitors. Nonetheless, one of the benefits of reading *Spatializing Culture* is the fertile uncovering of hidden dimensions of social dynamics and their conscious (or unknowing) reproduction by forces and behaviors not easily observable at first glance.

The book is in nine chapters. After the introduction and genealogies chapters, the core chapters of the book (chapters 3 through 8) are relatively similar, with comprehensive reviews of the literature and extended case studies aimed at illustrating some of the main concepts and contentious points. Chapters 3 and 4 are about the social production of space and social construction of space, respectively. Analyses of Parque Central in San José, Costa Rica, and the Silin Market in Taipei, Taiwan, illustrate the social production of space, while accounts of the historic erasure of the African American experience at Independence National Historic Park in Philadelphia and the reconstruction of post-war Beirut are utilized to exemplify the social construction of space. Chapter 5 sheds light on the relatively novel concept of embodied space. We are presented with three case studies on the dynamics of the body in motion via ritual walking and strolling through the examples of the decades-old *retreta* in San José, the *corso* in Serbia, and the now renamed Critical Mass bicycling event in Budapest—the latter somewhat provocative in its political potential as Low wisely recognizes.

Chapter 6 is centered on language, discourse, and space. The case studies of housing co-ops in the Mt. Pleasant neighborhood of Washington, D.C., and in New York City reveal the hurdles associated with filing applications and the experience of grueling financial vetting, which "people like us" go through in order to obtain a "decent and secure" place to live in the rather exclusive neighborhoods of these two global cities. Chapter 7 deals with emotion, affect, and space; the case studies cover how residents think about their gated communities and immediate hinterlands in New York and Texas as well as how a sample of mostly female individuals felt during the Egyptian revolution with its protests centered on Tahrir Square. Chapter 8 articulates notions of translocal space by engaging more directly with global space, nostalgia, and memories. The chapter's central theme is illustrated with the role of commerce and associated behaviors in mediating spatial, economic, social, cultural, and generational belonging with the case studies of Moore Street Market in Brooklyn, New York, and the Tachanah Merkasit in Tel Aviv, Israel.

Spatializing Culture appears to have accomplished its central goal of illustrating the distinction between social production and social construction of space and of expanding its analysis to the newer conceptual knowledge frames. While the genealogy is rather helpful for understanding and creating the conceptual scaffolding needed to analyze the various case studies, it seems to me that in most cases, space is thoroughly analyzed, but without a systematic explanation for how the ensuing place dynamics are or can be altered to resolve the newly unveiled societal dilemmas. To a certain extent, space and place remain limited to the fifth Venn diagram of (coterminous) relationship as these two are regularly asserted in the expression "ethnography of space and place." In a way, it is as if readers are responsible for making sense of the other four Venn diagram relationships: (i) separation of space and place, (ii) overlapping of space and place, (iii) place contained within space, and (iv) space contained within place.

Inspired by a recent call for mapping possibility in hopes of finding purpose and hope in community planning, I offer three thoughts on how to expand some of the analyses in *Spatializing Culture*.[1] I accept that these are departures from the mostly space ethnographies of the book, but I wish to push the envelope to include not only acting in the built environment but also resolving some of the established power dynamics so well identified by Low. First, the casual *passeo* in Latin American cities—also found in the unmentioned Barcelona *ramblas* and the pedestrian main streets and squares of Vienna, Austria— appears to be considered nonetheless across the Atlantic Ocean in Smederevska Palanka's *Corso* without acknowledgment of its replicability in, for instance, the larger territorial agglomeration of Belgrade's main pedestrian precinct of Kneza Mihaila. About ten years ago, I was rather surprised by the intense translocal globalizing effect that I saw when I walked away from the city's pedestrian precinct towards the new shining U.S. regional style shopping mall across the river, and, even more recently, when I read about the mega-redevelopment taking place on the city's waterfront, which will surely augment the diversion of customers away from the traditional downtown retail core.[2]

Second, the surveillance tower found in San José's Parque Central can also be found on the parking lots of several Latino supermarkets in suburban Phoenix, Arizona. In fact, there is a hidden dimension to scholarly discussions on housing preferences and typologies in the United States.[3] It is not only the fear of others—often supposed "illegal" immigrants—but how we feel about ourselves that makes us blindly believe in the power of walls, gates, guards, and the pandemic-induced use of plexiglass to protect us, when in reality neighbors within gated communities are likely to be as tantalizing as those who live in so-called non-CC&Rs ("covenants, conditions, and restrictions") neighborhoods.[4]

Third, city planners are often blamed for enabling changes in the built environment that benefit certain individuals more than others. However, many public markets in the U.S. have been either completely erased or partially replaced with bland supermarkets, which carry some ethnic products, no doubt, but have none of the cultural appeal, colorful display, traditional music, or typical smells found at the authentic ethnic markets—to a great extent with our collective connivance swayed by lower prices and unexamined lifestyles.[5] To Low's credit, the use of a Rapid Ethnographic Assessment Process (REAP) aimed at halting the conversion of Moore Street Market into an "affordable" housing development is laudable. On the other hand, the author's preference for a bus station in Israel is surprising when blocks away from her in the vicinity of CUNY's Graduate Center in midtown Manhattan was a Port Authority Bus Terminal, surely one of the busiest in the world. The development's multimodal nature, shopping assortment, long lines of waiting passengers, rapid aging condition, and proximity to Times Square could have also made for a rather illuminating ethnographic study.[6]

All in all, *Spatializing Culture: The Ethnography of Space and Place* constitutes a timely and important addition to the literature on Environment, Space, and Place. The breadth and depth of its theoretical analysis, coupled with the variety of case studies from places in four distinct regions of the planet, expressive maps and illustrations, and the thirty nine pages of references, provide plenty of "food for thought," and, I should add, avenues for further action in the classroom, library, conference center, city hall, town square, housing co-op, gated community, marketplace, bus station, airport, nature preserve, or spa.

NOTES

1. Leonie Sandercock, *Mapping Possibility: Finding Purpose and Hope in Community Planning* (New York: Routledge, 2023).
2. Ana Perić and Marija Maruna, "Post-Socialist Discourse of Urban Megaproject Development: From City on the Water to Belgrade Waterfront," *Cities* 130 (2022): 103876.
3. Torin Monahan, "Electronic Fortification in Phoenix: Surveillance Technologies and Social Regulation in Residential Communities," *Urban Affairs Review* 42, no. 2 (2006): 169–92.
4. Zygmunt Bauman, *Community: Seeking Safety in an Insecure World* (Cambridge: Polity Press, 2001).
5. Carlos J. L. Balsas, "The Role of Public Markets in Urban Habitability and Competitiveness," *Journal of Place Management and Development* 13, no. 1 (2019): 30–46.
6. Jan Gehl and Birgitte Svarre, *How to Study Public Life* (Washington, D.C.: Island Press, 2013).

NEW FROM MINNESOTA

The Lichen Museum
A. Laurie Palmer

"Draws attention to how lichens can offer new ways to think through questions of relationality, life and death, and our mutual obligations to each other." —**Heather Davis**, author of *Plastic Matter*

$24.95 paper | 184 pages | Art after Nature Series

Earth, Ice, Bone, Blood
Permafrost and Extinction in the Russian Arctic
Charlotte Wrigley

"Traverses issues fundamental to our time: the meanings of extinction, the experiences of earth-shaking change, the seductions of engineering both genetic and geological." —**Bathsheba Demuth**, author of *Floating Coast*

$22.95 paper | 256 pages

Noah's Arkive
Jeffrey J. Cohen and Julian Yates

"Magisterial yet wisely irreverent, *Noah's Arkive* touches upon urgent challenges, including ecofascism, decolonialization, and racial justice, while also delivering a learned, meticulously researched exhibit of historical ark narratives."
—**Stephanie LeMenager**, University of Oregon

$29.95 paper | 416 pages

Settling Nature
The Conservation Regime in Palestine-Israel
Irus Braverman

"A fascinating account of the formulation and enforcement of conservation policies in Palestine-Israel that examines a series of cases that exemplify tensions that emerge around attempts to conserve species, landscapes, and ecosystems." —**Harriet Ritvo**, author of *The Animal Estate*

$29.00 paper | 362 pages

Subsurface
Karen Pinkus

"Digging into the past to imagine a sustainable future, written with spark and wit, *Subsurface* is a welcome contribution to the environmental humanities." —**Verena Andermatt Conley**, Harvard University

$25.00 paper | 232 pages | Posthumanities Series, vol. 67

The Environmental Unconscious
Ecological Poetics from Spenser to Milton
Steven Swarbrick

"Offers an overlooked yet urgent mode of theorizing life beyond the human." —**Melissa E. Sanchez**, University of Pennsylvania

$28.00 paper | 346 pages